The Way I See It

The Way I See It

Life Lessons from a Child

Geneviève Hone

NOVALIS

© 2007 Novalis, Saint Paul University, Ottawa, Canada

Cover design and layout: Dominique Pelland
Cover artwork: Julien Mercure

Business Offices:
Novalis Publishing Inc.
10 Lower Spadina Avenue, Suite 400
Toronto, Ontario, Canada
M5V 2Z2

Novalis Publishing Inc.
4475 Frontenac Street
Montréal, Québec, Canada
H2H 2S2

Phone: 1-800-387-7164
Fax: 1-800-204-4140
E-mail: books@novalis.ca
www.novalis.ca

Library and Archives Canada Cataloguing in Publication

Hone, Geneviève
    The way I see it : life lessons from a child / Geneviève Hone.

ISBN-13: 978-2-89507-836-4
ISBN-10: 2-89507-836-X

    1. Child rearing. 2. Children–Conduct of life. 3. Values. 4. Moral
education. I. Title.

HQ772.5.H65 2007   649'.1   C2006-905358-8

Printed in Canada.

We acknowledge the financial support of the Government of Canada through the Book
Publishing Industry Development Program (BPIDP) for our publishing activities.

5 4 3 2 1   10 09 08 07

To Alex, who introduced me to this little boy

To our children and their loved ones,
whom our grandchildren are patiently educating

To Julien, who created the lovely painting for the cover

And in loving memory of our dearest friend, Dick Hanley

Acknowledgments

So many people, family and friends,

Have offered encouragement and help

While I was listening to the little boy who tells these stories.

You are too numerous to list here, but *I* know who you are.

And let me assure you that I will tell you again and again,

"Thank you from the bottom of my heart."

But I must say a special "thank you" to the Novalis team,

Especially Kevin Burns and Anne Louise Mahoney,

Who really know how to deal with two-and-a-half-year-olds

Whatever their age!

contents

Introduction

The little boy who tells these stories appeared out of a clear blue sky in August 2004. Perhaps I should say that he appeared out of a patch of clear blue sky located in the part of my brain that attempts to explain Life to myself and to other people. At first I dismissed him as a figment of my imagination, but he kept trying to get my attention again and again: during morning walks; during the "twilight zone," that strange period of time between sleep and wakefulness; during a drive through the countryside; during the preparation of a meal. At one point, he started asking that I respond to him, that I comment on what he was telling me, almost as if he wanted to make sure I was really listening. It got to the point that he would intrude into conversations I was having with family and friends, especially when we were talking about life: its hope, its pain, its mystery.

The little boy turned out to be somewhere between the ages of two and three, with many things to say. It took me quite a while to figure out who and what he is. He is not like any child I know, and yet, he reminds me of all the children I have known and learned to love through my experience as a mother, grandmother, social worker and family therapist. He keeps me on my toes: just when I think I understand how he thinks, he demonstrates another thinking style. Just when I think I understand how he feels, he surprises me with his capacity for insights and discoveries.

If this little boy is able to write about his life, it is because he has an astute grandmother who is able to understand what is not expressed clearly. In fact, he has two astute grandmothers, but one lives far away and he gets to see her less often. When she does visit, however, they have great discussions about all aspects of life while she pours love all over him. His "real" vocabulary is limited. A limited vocabulary can lead to all kinds of misunderstandings, as any seasoned traveller will tell you. When faced with the prospect of having to eat broccoli, a child's "NO WANT!" can hide many meanings. Perhaps it means "I'm saying 'no' because that's what I need to do at my age and anyway, you can't force me to swallow." Or, "Watch it, Daddy – when you are feeding me, you are not only giving me food, you are helping me develop my own relationship with food, so take it easy." Or "This stuff tastes really bad, and if you continue offering this kind of food, one of us will have to leave town." "NO WANT" definitely doesn't cut it. So the little boy's grandma has agreed to translate. She has assured him that nothing will be lost in translation. He suspects that, on the contrary, many extra things will have been *found* in translation!

His grandmother… It took me a while to figure out who she is, and I must say that I have not succeeded yet. As soon as I think I know where she's coming from, she changes her mind about something and affirms the contrary of what she was saying two days ago. She can suggest the wildest things, sometimes bordering on outrageous, and yet I get the impression that she is quite timid and hesitant. She is not like any grandmother I know, and yet she reminds me of all the grandparents and parents that I have met and learned to love through my experience as a parent and a therapist.

The little boy does not want his parents to know that he is writing this book, and that is why he is in the process of choosing a pseudonym. He and his grandmother firmly believe that parents have a right to peace and quiet, and he knows that having children is not particularly conducive to the acquisition of such a state. So he doesn't want his parents to be bothered by people ringing the doorbell and demanding to meet him and his friends. To this day, he has not revealed his real name to me, and I don't think he ever shall. But he has given me a hint: his real name does not begin with "c," that letter being reserved for "cat," as we all know.

1

Choosing to love:

Adoption

Allow me to introduce myself. Introducing myself is a bit complicated, since I do not want to tell you my name. I don't want my daddy and mommy to know that I am writing this, so my grandma said I should choose a pseudonym to tell my stories. I had no idea what a pseudonym was when Grandma first said that big word. For a second or two, I thought it might be the name of a brand of dinosaur that I hadn't met yet. But Grandma will never give me a big word without quickly explaining what it means – she's very careful about this. She knows that hearing new words all day long, all over the place, can be very annoying to children. New words are like puzzle pieces that you have to put together without even having a picture on the box. It can get complicated.

What I know so far about pseudonyms is that a pseudonym is like a Halloween mask, except it doesn't hide your face. It hides your name when you don't want to be recognized. Last Halloween, I often took off my mask so people could see that I am not really a big green ghost. They might not want to give candy to a big green ghost, so I helped them understand that there was a little boy under the green face. But I will not take off my pseudonym for you even if you offer lots of candy.

Since this conversation with Grandma, I have worked really hard to find the best new name for me. At first, I thought I would like to be known as Igor because of Prince Igor. Prince Igor is in a story that Grandma has been telling me, and this story will never end because I like it.

Grandma keeps changing the story to see if I'm listening. For instance, she'll say, "Prince Igor jumped on a train," but there are no trains in the story, just elephants and camels, and I have to say, "No train, Grandma, no train." The reason Grandma keeps changing the story is that she believes our own stories change all the time. Life can be very interesting if we let our stories change, but many people are taught that they are allowed only one story throughout their life and that their story can't be changed. This is very sad. Grandma wants me to get used to the idea that the story of my life is going to change over and over again. This way, I won't ever get bored.

After a while, I decided not to choose Igor as my pseudonym. Prince Igor has travelled to many countries and is very well known in those places, of course. I figured that if I ever visit those countries, there might be some confusion. So then I thought that Cracker Jack would make a nice name. Cracker Jack is a kind of popcorn that my friend Martin has tasted several times, and he tells me it is one of the best foods in the whole wide world. He likes it so much that he has never wanted to share some with me, so I have not tasted it, but I like the name. Cracker Jack sounds like a kind of firecracker and I like firecrackers. They remind me of fireworks, which I saw shining way up high in the sky when we went to the big birthday party for our country. One day I would like to learn how to drive fireworks.

But then again, after a while, I thought that people might think I look like a piece of popcorn with a name like that. So, I decided to change it. I considered several other new names, such as Crocodile, Elevator and Soccer, but none of these seemed to fit perfectly. I must confess at this point that I have not yet finalized my choice. Grandma thinks "Felix" would be a nice name, since it means "happy" and I am usually a happy child. She suggested that I try it on for size. Grandma says it's normal to want or need to change names once in a while, and it's normal to need time to find the name that suits you perfectly. It can take several tries. I'll let you know when I have completely made up my mind on this subject. For the time being, you can pretend my name is Felix. Don't worry about not knowing my real name. I don't know yours, either, but that won't prevent me from telling you things. So let's all relax about this whole name thing.

Now that the pseudonym matter is settled, I will tell you about Prince Igor. Prince Igor had a big treasure chest full of his favourite things. He even kept his teddy bear in it, which was a huge mistake because one day some bad people came and stole the treasure chest. I personally haven't met any bad people yet, but they are in many stories, and sometimes they can jump into your dreams right from the storybook and cause problems. Your parents have to wake you up in the middle of the night to pull the bad people away from you. That is a lot of work for them, and they get very tired. You can tell in the morning by your parents' faces when they have done a lot of work during the night: they walk around slowly and they don't say much even when they do talk. Try to put them in quiet surroundings, perhaps in the kitchen so they can make breakfast. This may also be a good time to offer to watch your favourite show in the other room to help them get some peace and quiet.

I really like Prince Igor. He is very brave as he travels all over the world to find his teddy bear. He would never abandon his bear. I used to worry about his teddy bear, but Grandma said that as long as somebody is looking for you and really wants to find you, you will be all right. Sometimes I pretend that I'm Prince Igor.

Grandma thinks I have lots of interesting things to say, and I believe her because she always listens to me very carefully when I tell her a story. She offered to write down the stories that I tell her because they would interest a great many people. I accepted her help because I can't yet write in words that big people understand. Mind you, I like to write – it's a good hobby. And I have written many times on my blackboard, in my colouring books, and occasionally on the walls of my bedroom. It's mostly drawings, though, rather than letters.

Like Prince Igor, I have a teddy bear, but I make sure never to put him in my treasure chest. I have other friends, too. We meet and discuss things when our parents are talking among themselves during a visit or when we are involved in some kind of educational activity or playgroup. An educational activity is something our parents have us do when they are tired of being everything they have to be to be good parents: swim instructor, librarian, music teacher, museum curator, occupational therapist, art instructor, gym teacher, singing teacher, cook, chauffeur, nurse, pharmacist, doctor, etc. I generally like educational activities and playgroups. They are a good way to meet my friends and expand my mind, as Grandma explained to me.

But enough about me. Let me tell you about what happened to my friends and me last week at playgroup. We were happily going on with our lives. I had discovered a very nice playdough station and I was making pizza for the group. Ahn-Lin had decided she would make healthy cookies with the playdough and was working in the kitchen corner. Martin then decided he would be the one who would actually bake the cookies, and he told Ahn-Lin to move over. Well, Ahn-Lin didn't agree with that idea at all, and she pushed Martin away. Martin started kicking the oven, though the oven had done nothing wrong. The playgroup teacher came over and had Martin go into another area to take a few moments to reflect on the pros and cons of kicking. We all went back to our work.

Martin was allowed to move again eventually, but I could tell that he wasn't too happy with the way he had been treated. So when he joined us, he told Ahn-Lin right to her face that she was adopted. Ahn-Lin looked at him like he was a boring movie and went on with her baking. Eric and I were not too impressed at first, mainly because we didn't know what "adopted" meant, but then Martin explained that Ahn-Lin's parents were not her real parents. Well, I had seen Ahn-Lin's parents that very morning when they brought her to playgroup and they were very real, as far as I could tell. I said that to Martin, but Martin said that her real parents were in a faraway land – the ones I saw this morning are her not-real parents. Her not-real parents had travelled in a big airplane to go and get her. When they got to the faraway land, Ahn-Lin was already a big baby and that is why she is older than the rest of us and completely toilet-trained. I think Martin is a bit jealous of Ahn-Lin because she has already taken a plane ride and he hasn't.

I like Ahn-Lin. She is nice and always willing to share her toys with us, so I was sorry to learn that her parents were not really real. It must be hard to have not-real parents. I asked Ahn-Lin to tell me more about her faraway land, as Prince Igor is visiting there this week, but she suggested that I get back to my pizzas.

When I reported the news to Grandma, she remained calm. I could tell she was not too impressed by what Martin had said, even though she is aware that Martin has two daddies and therefore knows many more things than I do. Grandma said that Ahn-Lin's parents were very real. I had been right to say so to Martin. Grandma suggested that a more useful way of thinking about this whole situation would be to think that Ahn-Lin had a first set of parents who were very real. They are the parents who made her be born. But then something happened, we don't know what, that made it impossible for them to take care of Ahn-Lin. They did what they had to do to have Ahn-Lin taken to a place where her second set of parents could find her. The second set of parents is as real as the first ones – the fact that they chose her makes them real parents. That's how they came to adopt her. A person could have many sets of parents throughout their life, and all these parents would be real if they have chosen to love that person.

Grandma, who likes to be precise, added that all parents must adopt their children and that Mommy and Daddy, though I didn't know it, are constantly adopting me – that is, choosing to be with me. They have to keep on doing that because I change all the time. Part of me is always like a little stranger to them, so they have to adopt this little stranger over and over again. They don't have to take an airplane, but they have to travel to faraway places inside their hearts to be able to adopt me.

So when Daddy came home, I told him that I knew I was adopted. He looked up at the ceiling like he does sometimes when he hears about things I have done during the day, and he said to Mommy that he would have to scold Grandma. But then he laughed, and I knew that this time Grandma would get away with it.

"we dreamed of you"

we dreamed of you.

we dreamed of the day we would finally meet you

And reach out to you, touch you and love you.

One day, our dream came true.

we travelled halfway across our country,

Halfway across the world,

Halfway across your country,

And finally, at last, you were ours to cherish forever.

After all those travels, we thought we would stay home

To get to know you and love you even more

And help you grow and learn and embrace life

To become as beautiful as you are.

We did stay home
But you sent us right on our way again.
And since we have you
We travel right through our minds, our souls
         and our hearts
To find you, touch you and love you.
There seems to be no end to the travelling
         you have us do.

You are the best travel agent ever!

2

Being together in sorrow:

The lost baby

I must tell you what happened to Stefan. He comes to our library activity because he likes books with dinosaurs, and there are quite a few there. About a month ago, he came to the group with his grandmother instead of his mother. He told us that his mommy had gone to the hospital with his daddy to get their new baby, and on the way back, they lost the baby. Everybody was crying at his house except for his mommy. Stefan was upset because nobody was looking for the baby that was lost. He was afraid that if he got lost, nobody would look for him. I was very interested because of Prince Igor searching for his teddy bear, and I told Stefan that maybe the baby had been taken by the bad people to the faraway lands. Martin said no, that was not it at all. Martin has two daddies, as I may have mentioned, and he likes to share his opinions with others since he has so many. Because of that we listen to him most of the time, and also because he is taller than we are. Martin said the baby had not been lost, he had just been put away somewhere. When Martin was in the habit of throwing his toy engine through the living room, his mother would say, "If you do that again, you are going to lose your engine for good." Well one day, this is exactly what happened, and Martin's mother put the toy engine in the basement closet. (I notice that when adults say "for good," they usually mean "for bad.")

Anyway, Stefan agreed that this was probably what had happened. Then we didn't see him for a while. But we heard two mothers talking. One said that Stefan's family was going through a rough time and that Stefan was not feeling well. We were a bit worried because it's good to worry about your friends. But then we forgot about it because there were new movies that our mothers could borrow for us from the library.

Stefan came back last week, and this time he brought his mommy. He had quite a story to tell. He told us that he first thought the lost baby had probably been put into the closet in the basement like Martin's toy engine. During the night, the lost baby would jump from the closet into Stefan's dreams and Stefan's daddy had to wake him up to pull the baby away from him. Night after night, the baby just kept jumping right back in and Stefan's daddy had to wake him up again and again. So Stefan decided not to go to his playroom in the basement because that's where the basement closet was. His daddy tried to get him to go downstairs by going down with him, but that made Stefan scream even more. Stefan's mommy tried to help by holding and rocking him, but though she was warm on the outside, there was some ice inside of her – Stefan could tell by her eyes. Stefan didn't like that at all. Ice is good when there is a Popsicle around it, but there is also bad ice. This was not a good ice.

Stefan tried to warm his mother up by cuddling even closer, but that didn't help much.

Finally, Stefan's mommy and daddy brought him to see a new doctor because he was screaming too much. Stefan's daddy explained that this doctor was going to listen to Stefan's heart, but he would just use his ears and not the magic circle with the tubes that go into the ears. The doctor listened to Stefan's parents explain about the screaming. Then he said to Stefan, "Do you think the lost baby was put into the basement closet?" Stefan said yes. Then the doctor said, "The baby is not lost and the baby is not in the closet, Stefan. The baby died." Stefan knew exactly what the doctor was talking about because he once had found a dead baby bird. Stefan's daddy had explained that the dead bird couldn't move because its life had gone out of it, and then they had put the bird in a hole in the ground under a tree. Life is what makes dead birds move before they are dead. The doctor turned to Stefan's mommy and suggested something for her to say to Stefan. So Stefan's mommy looked at Stefan and said, "Thank you for trying to help, Stefan." And then she burst into tears. It was as if all the ice was melting and coming out of her eyes. And right then, Stefan knew that his mommy would be warm inside once more and that the lost baby would never jump into his dreams again.

I sure was looking forward to telling Grandma this very sad story because she likes stories where people help each other. I needed some explanation on how Stefan's screaming had helped his mommy. I have some experience with screaming, since I occasionally use this approach when my parents are not behaving according to my standards. When I do, my mommy always says, "Screaming is not helping you at all at this time."

Grandma explained that families have parents and children; that is the natural order of things. I already knew that, of course. What I didn't know is that families try to be together in such a way that the parents are always the big people and that the children are always the little people. When something painful happens to the parents, they don't have the energy to be big people all the time, and the children sense this even if nobody ever talks about it. So children, even if they don't quite know what they are doing, will often do something to make the parents become big people once again. It doesn't necessarily look like a big help. In fact, it often seems that what the children are doing adds to the problem. But it is an honest effort on the part of the children to say, "We need a family where the parents are *big* people." Grandma thinks that that is what Stefan was doing, and his mommy understood that when she thanked him for his help.

Grandma also didn't think that this story was a sad story. She said that it is a story about sadness and people being sad because they lost someone precious, and that is different. She also explained that people – and this includes me since Grandma thinks of me as a people – each have their own way of dealing with painful things. Some people need to spend lots of time inside themselves to find their own way, and they may then appear to be closed to the rest of the world. But they are not really; it's just that they need to protect their way of getting better. Other people need to spend time with loved ones to talk about their anger, their sadness and their fear. And others need to keep busy, often to the point that people around them are tempted to tell them to slow down and rest. Keeping busy might be their way of slowly coming to terms with their loss. It's a bit like when I need to sleep because I am very tired, but I am too tired to go to sleep. It's my body's way of dealing with being tired, and it may seem a bit strange that I just don't fall into sleep easily then. My parents try to help me because they know that I am doing the best I can.

At this point, I must admit that I was becoming a bit sleepy, since this conversation went on at bedtime. I reminded Grandma that we must get back to Prince Igor. It so happened that Prince Igor himself had had a very long day travelling in the faraway lands, so I fell asleep while he was getting ready to sleep in a house that he had built in a big tree to be safe from the bad people.

"I gave you life and you took it"

I gave you life and you took it

Right into your tiny hands and your tiny heart

And you smiled and laughed and danced.

I kept giving you life and you took it

Right into your little hands and your little heart

And you crawled and walked and ran.

I kept giving you life and you took it

Right into your strong hands and your strong heart

And you wondered and talked and sang.

And then the dark clouds came,

And hid my time, my energy, my love, and my life

With loss and sorrow and anger and fear.

I didn't feel I could go on giving you life

And yet somehow I must have continued

Because you opened your loving hands

     and your loving heart

And gave life right back to me.

3

Growing fast:

The big brother

David has a new baby in his house. David is three years old, so of course he knows all about where babies come from. His mother had given him ample warning that he would be having a new sister, but she was tired so she forgot to tell him a couple of important things. For one thing, she never told him that even if her tummy was shaped like a big round ball, the baby would not have that shape. So David had to forget his plans to bounce the baby all around the house. The other thing that was not clearly spelled out was that his new sister was going to stay for a very long time, longer than eleventeen Christmases, even. So when his little sister didn't go away after a few days, like other visitors did, David very politely inquired when she would be leaving. He was shocked to learn that she wouldn't be.

To complicate matters, David discovered that he really did not enjoy at all having a little sister and being a big boy. Becoming a big boy is something that we all have to do eventually, unless of course you are a girl, but it is not something we look forward to as much as our parents do. Personally, I am not yet a big boy, though my mommy and my daddy like to pretend I am. They say to their friends, "Felix is such a big boy now, we have had to buy him new shoes again, and he can count to thirteen." I am in absolutely no hurry to take this giant step of becoming a big boy. At the most, I would consider becoming a medium boy, and this only on a part-time basis, and only if my parents let me watch TV before going to daycare in the morning. Grandma says that I could be a great negotiator when I grow up, but this won't happen because I am in no mood to grow up, especially after what happened to David.

So, one morning at playgroup while the mommies in our group were talking together and taking turns rocking David's little sister and saying gooey things like, "Oh, she's so precious," we made plans to help David. Eugenia, who is a girl and therefore knows about little sisters though she has a little brother, said that maybe David's mommy really liked little babies. When David had begun to grow up, she knew she wouldn't have a baby to play with. So that's why she and David's daddy had decided get a new one. Then Martin, who always has many opinions because he has two daddies and two big brothers, said that if David stopped being a big boy and became a baby once more, his mommy wouldn't need the little sister and would send her back where she came from. It wasn't quite clear to any of us where exactly the little sister had come from, but that wasn't important.

So David decided to become a baby again. When he and his mother returned home, the first thing he did was to immediately untoilet-train himself. Then he couldn't drink from a cup anymore. He took the baby's pacifier and gave it to his teddy bear, though David doesn't really have a teddy bear. He has a teddy dinosaur that his daddy brought back from a trip. His dinosaur has big, big teeth and it can yell pretty loud and it ripped the pacifier with its teeth. When his mommy would call him to come to the table for dinner, David would fall on the floor and be unable to get up. His daddy had to pick him up, since his mommy was always holding the baby. And then, David couldn't remember how to put his arms through his pyjama sleeves or how to use his fork, and he would accidentally spill his apple juice on his head. He would cry, exactly like his little sister, when his daddy put him to bed.

David worked really hard at becoming a baby once more, but no one seemed to appreciate his efforts. His daddy kept picking him off the floor and his mommy kept holding the baby sister. Everybody kept pretending that there was only one baby in the family. Both his mommy and his daddy kept reminding him that he was a *big boy now* and offered him many opportunities to act like one. For instance, his daddy brought him to the farm museum to see the tractors, and David almost forgot he was too little to sit on the big tractor.

David could tell that his parents didn't understand that he had become a baby once more: they kept treating him like a big boy, no matter what. It was very difficult for David, as it is for all three-year-olds when they have parents who, for one reason or another, just can't see what is obvious. David's mommy is a very good mommy in spite of having invited this baby to stay at their house, so she kept saying to David that she loved him, and she would rock him and sing lullabies to him at bedtime. But during the day, she always called David her big boy, and that didn't help matters.

After several days of misunderstanding, David's mommy finally caught on to the fact that there were now two babies in the house. She likes babies, so she was happy about that, David could tell. She stopped insisting that David was a big boy, and she started calling him her really little boy, which was very nice. She was not mocking David; she just recognized that he was as little as the new baby, but in a different way. She stopped talking about the untoilet-training events and insisting that David eat with his own fork. She even gave David his own baby bottle from which he could drink his milk. She wrapped him in baby blankets when he was watching TV. All kinds of things like that. Even David's daddy let him be a baby, but that doesn't count because David's daddy and mommy always make plans together. David couldn't tell if his daddy was just going along with the idea or if he sincerely realized that the family now had two babies.

David told us at our next meeting how well his plan had worked, but I could tell that he was not totally happy with his new role. He pretended to be a baby only when his mother was looking at him. When she was busy with the other mothers saying gooey things to the baby sister, he acted as grown-up as he really was, and he threw a library book across the room to prove it. When I discussed this with Grandma, she explained that David was learning new things through this experiment, and that the experiment was not quite finished yet. She said that when people try new approaches to their lives, they can be quite excited and happy, but they can also be worried and unhappy at the same time. This is normal; it just shows that they are alive.

The following week, David decided that his parents had learned their lesson, and it was time to become a big boy again. Plus, he wanted to be able to drive the big tractor at the farm museum. He retoilet-trained himself, which was easy because he hadn't forgotten how things go. He insisted that he be given back his fork and spoon and his regular drinking cup, and he retrieved the pacifier from his teddy dinosaur to give it back to his mommy. After one look at the pacifier, David's mommy said that the teddy dinosaur could keep it.

When I reported this to Grandma, she said that when people grow up, they keep in their hearts, their heads, and all over their bodies, the capacity to be little. Everybody needs to feel and act little every once in a while. This is what helps them experience joy and creativity, for one thing. It also helps them realize that they need help with certain aspects of their lives, such as when they are ill. It is all right to ask for help and receive it. Grandma says that my grandpa always knows that when she is afraid of something that's not really dangerous, it's just because she is a little bit little. Grandpa doesn't scold her at all. He just stays with her long enough for her to start being a big person again, and Grandma says that this helps her a lot. It's a lot faster than if she had to prove to him that it's all right to be little. She says that in spite of everything, most people want to grow up.

"I will tell no one"

I will tell no one.

Cross my heart and hope to die

As you used to say when you were six.

I didn't tell when you were four and ten and fifteen
and twenty.

I didn't tell when you were thirty and forty.

And I won't tell when you are fifty and sixty
and seventy

Unless my aging brain makes me give away the secret

That I don't want to tell, to anyone, ever.

Even when you are very big and strong
Even when you are very old and wise
And have helped conquer space and had a star
            named after you,
And have discovered the cure for the most mysterious
            disease in the world
And saved millions of people,
And have written the book that offers the definitive
            answer to Life's mystery,
And have solved the theorem that has plagued
            mathematicians for centuries,
And have loved and loved again and shared your love
            with all who suffer,
I will not tell.

I will not tell that, to me, you are still little,

And that in my heart you have kept exactly the place

That you occupied when I first met you,

When you were so little and the world was so big.

4

Dealing with fragility:

The baby who choked

I don't think I've ever told you about Liam, who comes to our playgroup once in a while. Liam doesn't talk much, but I'll tell you, the last time we saw him, he had quite a story to tell. The story was already over once we heard about it, so we didn't get the chance to discuss things with him and help him. But I think it did him good to talk about it. Grandma often says that it helps people to talk about things to their friends or their family. But when she babysits me she doesn't let me talk that much at bedtime after she's read me my stories and sung me my lullabies. She says, "Felix, it'll keep. You can talk about that tomorrow."

What happened is this: Liam and his mommy were at home with their little baby who is not so little anymore since she can crawl and stand up and fall down all by herself. But they still think of her as a little baby, which she is, of course, compared to Liam, who his now two and a half or three years old. A neighbour came by for a cup of coffee, and she and Liam's mother were talking. All of a sudden, they heard a funny noise, and they saw that the little baby was making funny noises from her throat, and she was a funny colour. As it turned out, though, there was nothing funny about the situation. The little baby had crawled to the family room and had found a piece of popcorn underneath the sofa, and she had tried to eat it but she couldn't swallow it. Liam's mommy picked up the baby and started crying, "Oh, God!" over and over, but the baby still didn't know how to chew the popcorn. Then the neighbour took the baby from Liam's mommy and turned her inside out, and out came the piece of popcorn with some leftover juices. The baby started crying and Liam's mommy and the neighbour did, too. After a while Liam joined in because it seemed the thing to do.

This story is not about popcorn as such, and there is more to come. But I would like to say at this point that I have not yet had the privilege of eating popcorn. My mommy likes to introduce one food at a time, and apparently there are more introductions to be made before we get to popcorn. I know, however, that popcorn smells extremely good. Sometimes when I'm already in bed, my parents make popcorn and they let the smell come up to my room to remind me that I should be asleep and not smelling this at all. I am just saying this to make sure that everyone understands that popcorn is not necessarily bad for your throat.

After Liam's dinner that evening, his daddy came home and he was very upset. Liam could tell this right away by the way his daddy didn't say hello to him. He went directly to Liam's mommy and said, "What's this I hear? We talked on the phone this afternoon and you didn't even have the guts to tell me that the baby almost choked to death. If I hadn't run into the neighbour outside, I suppose I would never have heard about this. I told you over and over again that the cleaning lady is not doing her job. We should have let her go ages ago, but you insisted that you liked her – and look what happened."

Liam's mommy became all white in the face and her eyes became small and really pointed and she hollered, "Well, if you were at home more often, maybe you could check under the sofas to make sure that everything is as clean as you like it. But all I hear from you is work, work and work." And she rushed into the bathroom. And then Liam's daddy put his coat back on and he went outdoors. He slammed the door so hard that it hurt Liam's ears and also his heart. Liam's mommy then came out of the bathroom to tell Liam he could watch a movie. Liam chose the longest one he had in case his parents exploded again.

When the movie got to the part that Liam doesn't like because the animals attack the baby lion's daddy, he climbed on the sofa to look out the window. He saw his daddy walking back and forth in front of the house. After a while, his daddy came back in and said to Liam's mommy, "You know, I was so scared when I heard that the baby had choked, that all I felt like doing was finding someone to blame. I shouldn't have done that. I'm really sorry." Liam's mommy started to cry and said, "When you are afraid, you blame me. When I am afraid, I blame me. I just can't stand it anymore." So his parents went to the other room to talk about things, as they like to do after having exploded. Liam got to watch the whole movie, and that helped him somewhat because his tummy was trembling a bit and he had sort of a sore throat. Later on, his daddy put him to bed, but during the night Liam was attacked by a big truck full of purple popcorn, and his mommy had to wake him up to pull the truck away from him.

We could tell that Liam was still a bit shaken up by the explosion, but we didn't know what to say to him. Even Martin didn't know what to say. So we said nothing, but I let Liam sit on the red cushion that I usually reserve for myself. I told the group that I would ask Grandma how we might help Liam and that I would report back. I must confess right away that the following week, I completely forgot to report back because there was a clown at playgroup making animals out of balloons.

Grandma said that most of the time, when someone tells you an important story, such as a story about an explosion, you don't have to say much. You can just stay there and listen carefully. When you do this, the other person feels better because you are not being critical. Apparently this is a very good way of helping, even though you might feel that you aren't doing anything. Small gestures, such as letting Liam sit on my cushion (even though it was only two and a half minutes before I took it back), may also help.

Grandma knows a lot about explosions because she used to work with people who exploded regularly. She noticed that many times, explosions happen just before people make an important change for the better. It's as if they are letting go, suddenly, of all kinds of things that they don't need to be or do anymore. The important thing is that people learn something about themselves and others after exploding. I could understand that because Prince Igor once stepped into a volcano by accident and he learned never to go near a volcano again, at least not until he had found his teddy bear.

Grandma also explained that many good people tend to blame themselves when they make a mistake, especially if they have been taught that they must do things perfectly and that making a mistake is bad. Worse than that, many good people tend to blame themselves for accidents or things that are totally out of their control. So it is useless to blame good people who have made a mistake or have had an accident because they are already blaming themselves. It's a big waste of time, energy and intelligence. I must remember to explain that to my mommy the next time I make a mistake and throw my toy engine across the room by accident.

"I remember exactly how my life was"

I remember exactly how my life was

Before I had you.

I was alive and so busy

Inventing all sorts of things

And discovering the mysteries of the world.

I was braving obstacles and conquering demons.

And I was growing and learning again and again.

My life was filled with hope and joy.

I am still alive and busy

Inventing things and discovering mysteries.

I am still braving obstacles and conquering demons

And growing and learning as I did before I had you.

My life is still filled with hope and joy.

Yet why is everything so different

Now that I do have you?

Because I know,

Though I can't bear to think it,

Though I can't bear to feel it,

That it could happen that I don't have you anymore.

5

Forming a community:

The abused child

Last week at the library, Sophie was there with her mother and a big girl who looked really weird. We learned that the big girl's name is Melanie. She is seven years old or something, or maybe eleventeen. I can't remember exactly. Melanie was sitting behind the singing circle, and I could tell that she wasn't too interested in singing about a spider who went up a spout. She just sat there sort of rocking herself and chewing on a piece of her hair, and she never smiled even when we sang "The Happy Song." She looked a bit scary, I must add, so I decided not to get too close to her.

Sophie told us that Melanie is staying at Sophie's house with Sophie's mommy and daddy and her big sister Sarah and their dog. (I'm sorry I don't remember the dog's name, I just know that it isn't Spot. Dogs are important people, and we should remember their names, so I'll get the information for you.) Melanie will be staying at Sophie's house for a while till Melanie's mommy gets better. When I heard that, I thought her mommy was sick, but it turns out that her mommy had been a bad mommy to Melanie, so Melanie had to go live somewhere else. As I have not met any bad people yet, I was a bit surprised to learn that some live close by. I was also frightened because Prince Igor's teddy bear was stolen by bad people, and perhaps Melanie's mommy was one of them. I don't really know what bad people look like. Luckily, my teddy bear was safe at home: he does not come with me in the car unless we travel to visit my Granny, the grandmother who is not Grandma.

Sophie told us that Melanie's daddy is working on a ship in a faraway land. I was interested to hear about that because that's precisely where Prince Igor is travelling this week. Perhaps he will meet Melanie's daddy. But Melanie's daddy won't be coming back to live with Melanie's mommy because he is going to live with another mommy that he found in the faraway land. When she heard about that, Melanie's mommy stopped being happy and became angry with Melanie because Melanie missed her daddy and kept asking when he would be coming home. Then Melanie's mommy turned into one of the bad people and started hurting Melanie. In those days Melanie used to go to school, but then she began hating school and she hit some younger children in the schoolyard. The teacher called Melanie's mother and discovered that Melanie's mother was a bad mommy and that she had a drinking problem. That's how Melanie came to live with Sophie and her family. I must add here that I used to have a drinking problem myself, but that's behind me now. My mommy helped me by not giving me juice or water after dinner, to help me stay dry through the night.

That day, as we were leaving the library, my mommy waved to Melanie. Melanie looked at her and didn't smile or even wave back. Then my mommy said, "You know, Felix, this is the first time that Melanie has come to the activity at the library. She might be a little afraid of all these people she doesn't know. It would be nice if you waved to her to say hello." I was a bit surprised by this suggestion, since my mommy had already waved to Melanie and it hadn't worked. So I waved with my two hands to make sure Melanie saw me. Melanie did see me, and she laughed a little bit and gave a wave back with just her fingers. Maybe her hands hurt because of her mommy. My mommy laughed and said that a good-looking guy like me will make any girl smile.

Grandma was very interested by this story, since she likes stories where people have the chance to get better. But then she told me something strange. She said, "Maybe Melanie's mommy is not a bad person at all. Maybe she is a good person who is acting like a bad person because she doesn't know what else to do. Sometimes good people do bad things, like hitting somebody, because their heart and their head feel like they are all broken up. I don't think we should say that Melanie's mommy is a bad person. Maybe we should say that she is calling for help."

I didn't agree with this. I know about calling for help. In one of my movies, the children look for a prince who has been locked up in a dungeon. They know where to find him because he says, "Help me… Help me…" Also, my mommy has taught me to say, "Help me" when I have problems with my toys. I said Melanie's mommy had a strange way of calling for help. Grandma had to agree with that – it would seem easier just to ask for help, but sometimes people don't know how to do that. To make me understand, she reminded me that occasionally I have thrown my toy engine across the room when my mommy didn't immediately answer my call for help with the train tracks. I must admit that I may have done that once or twice, sort of by accident, but that was when I was little and I didn't understand about parents' right to talk on the phone in peace.

Now that we understood each other, Grandma gave me another important piece of information. She said that inside each person, there is some bad and there is some good. The good and the bad are fighting to see who will be bigger. Those we call good people often have had other people help their good side win. Those we call bad people often have not had that chance. Maybe Melanie's mother did not have enough people to help her good side win. It's very important, Grandma said, to form communities where people can watch out for each other and give help when needed. She explained that my parents give help when they leave food in the Food Bank bin at the grocery store. They receive help when they talk with other parents and get ideas from them about how to take care of me. When my friends and I discuss things together we are also being a community. When my mommy suggested that I wave to Melanie, she knew that Melanie needs to know that she is part of a community. Saying hello to her will help her know that she is not alone. A community helps you see better what you are seeing already, and it helps you begin to see things that you are not seeing yet but that would help if you could see them.

When Grandma starts saying things like what she just said about the community helping you to see, I begin to feel a little sleepy, especially if it's my bedtime. This discussion was getting long, and I was afraid that we wouldn't have time to see what happened to Prince Igor, who was stuck in the desert with only a camel for a community. So we ended the discussion, but Grandma said we would get back to it one day because the problem of good and evil has not yet been solved in this world, though she has been working on it for a very long time.

"Send love to ten
of your friends"

Send love to ten of your friends

And they in turn will send love to ten of their friends

who in turn will each send love to ten of their friends

And in a little while

You will start receiving huge quantities of love.

Do not break this chain.

People who have broken it have lost many precious

things and people

And have lived to dearly regret having broken the chain.

I repeat: Do not break this chain.

I sent love to all my friends

And even to people I barely knew

Because love must go round and round.

And I received huge quantities of love,

But none from you, my friend, my lover, my partner.

You wrote that you now belonged to another chain of love

One that I could not join.

I did not break the chain of love, and yet I lost you.

I also lost myself

And began turning round and round in a world

     too big for just me

That no love could fill.

Then, one day, this child who is still our child,

This child who knows love and spreads it

     all over the place

Reached out to me to start a new chain of love

And the world became just the right size once more.

6

Bumping into each other:

The great temper tantrum

My memory is not what it will be once I grow up and develop more brain cells, so I'm not certain if I've told you about the Great Temper Tantrum that we had the privilege to witness last month at the library. The reason I mention my memory is to have you understand that children need to have things repeated to them often, especially things that concern good behaviour and rules. My mommy often says to me, "For the eleventeenth time, Felix, would you please not bang your fork on the table?" I notice that when parents pronounce "please" as if they were saying it for the first time ever and really needed to get all the letters in one at a time, they really mean "or else." But not banging forks on the table, though it is considered by many to be good manners, is not a rule that particularly interests little children, for obvious reasons. Let's just say that it's not something I would make a conscious effort to remember.

But I shall remember, even when I am as old as Grandma, the temper tantrum that Martin threw in the activity room. I thought I could throw decent tantrums – my mommy even describes them as "big" – but I must tell you that Martin has developed techniques that I could never have imagined. (Martin is our friend who has two daddies, two brothers and two bedrooms, and therefore knows twice as much about raising children as the rest of us do. I admire him greatly, though in the reading circle I make sure that my mommy is seated between him and me.) The whole thing started when we were invited to get a shaker from the big basket to prepare for "The Happy Song." Martin, who likes to have two of most things because that's how it's done in his family, decided he wanted to have two shakers of each colour. Since there were not enough shakers to fill his needs, he took Ahn-Lin's shaker away from her without even saying "please." To tell the whole truth – though Grandma says that the "whole truth" rarely exists – even if Martin had said "please," it would have sounded like a big "or else." Martin's mommy then told him to give the shaker back to Ahn-Lin and say, "Sorry." That didn't fit into Martin's plans at all.

The whole thing was just like a big explosion, without the smoke but with extra noise. It went so fast I can't really describe it, but I can tell you there were several kicks all over the place, including one on Martin's mommy's leg, some attempts at biting, some rolling on the floor, a shoe flying off a foot, and hollering. Hollering is like shouting, except you use your whole body to do it. Hollering is major and can be quite frightening to the hollerer. I have not hollered more than once or twice, but I remember being very tired afterwards.

Everybody was looking at the explosion, even the library lady who forgot to lead us into "The Happy Song." I grabbed the red cushion I like to reserve for myself and hung on to my mommy. I needed to hang on a bit because the vibrations from the explosion made my tummy tremble a little. And then we saw Martin's mommy grow a lot taller all of a sudden. She picked Martin up, kicks and all, and walked out of the room. The library lady told us to sit down again and had us sing the song about the spider going up a spout. She could tell nobody was in the mood for "The Happy Song." Spiders going up and down fit the situation better. I got hold of Martin's yellow cushion to save it for him, and also because an extra cushion is helpful when you have a trembly tummy. But Martin didn't come back to the group that day.

Grandma was very interested in this story because she has worked a lot with people who exploded quite often. She explained that our lives are made up of lots and lots of stories that go on all day long. For instance, when I brush my teeth at night, I am in the middle of a little story that is called "preparing for bed," and when I am very slowly putting on my boots, I am in the middle of a little story called "preparing to go outside because it's good for my health." While I am in the middle of a story, every other person is also in the middle of a story that is not my story. This part I could understand easily because of Prince Igor, who is always in the middle of a story. It's nice to know that the story will never end, even after he has found his teddy bear. I am mentioning this to reassure you that Prince Igor *will* find his teddy bear. It's just a matter of time and travel.

The rest of what Grandma said is a little harder to understand, so I'm telling this part very slowly. It seems that people's stories bump into each other all day long, all over the world. Some stories bump gently into each other and it's a nice bump. They say, "Oh, there you are. I'm glad to have bumped into you." Other stories bump into each other and it's not as gentle, but it's still okay. They say, "Oh there you are. I'm sorry I've bumped into you a bit roughly. In case we bump into each other again, let's learn to be gentle about it." And then there are stories that bump into each other and hurt each other. They say, "Oh, there you are. You do not belong here. I shall have to do something very forceful to make you understand that you must never bump into me again." And that's when you have an explosion.

Grandma told me that even things that are not people seem to have their own story. For example, Grandma's hands hurt easily because she has used them too often to do fun things, so when she tries to open a new jar of peanut butter, the story of her hands bumps into the story of the peanut butter jar, which is trying to remain sealed for hygienic purposes. Please do not ask me what "hygienic purposes" means. I haven't a clue. But I understand about things having stories that bump into mine. When you are my age, life is full of things like TVs, cereal boxes, winter boots and high light switches all having their own stories that bump into your story. They are all over the place, these stories.

Grandma said we don't know what Martin's story was when the explosion happened, and maybe he didn't either, since we can't always keep up with our own stories. But we know that he *was* in the middle of some story and that the story was probably not about an explosion, but about something else that Martin thought would be good for him. Perhaps his story was that he wanted to experiment with doing "The Happy Song" with a large number of shakers, and that story bumped into Ahn-Lin's story, which was about finally being able to obtain a purple shaker. Martin's story certainly crashed into his mommy's story, which was about trying to teach Martin to be considerate.

Then Grandma went on to say that life is made up of stories bouncing off each other, and that is what makes life so interesting. This gave me the opportunity to suggest she tell me another part of Prince Igor's story. Well, would you believe it? It so happened that Prince Igor's story of trying to get into the Sheik's castle to retrieve his teddy bear crashed right into the story of the Sheik, who was trying to keep the teddy bear for himself because he had never had a teddy bear of his own. He had just had a teddy camel, and because of the humps, teddy camels are never cuddly enough to take care of you when your tummy is trembly.

"I was walking through my life"

I was walking through my life
Going in my own direction
Looking straight ahead
Eyes fixed on my destiny.
You were walking through your life
Going in your own direction
Looking straight ahead
Eyes fixed on your destiny.

And all of a sudden, we bumped into each other.
"Sorry, I didn't mean that."
And we quickly averted our eyes
To continue walking towards what had seemed
       our destiny.
But once again, we bumped into each other.
"Sorry, I didn't mean to."

Again and again, we bumped into each other
Till finally, one of us, I can't remember which,
Or perhaps it was the two of us, said,
"Actually, I'm not sorry at all. I'm rather enjoying this."
And the other one, or perhaps it was the two of us, said,
"Why don't we walk in the same direction,
Eyes fixed on a shared destiny?
This way, we won't keep bumping into each other."

Since then, we have walked in the same direction,

Eyes fixed on a shared destiny,

Yet we keep bumping into each other

In joy and pain, anger and forgiveness,

Fear and trust, war and peace.

But never again have we said to each other,

"I'm sorry I bumped into you."

7

Tolerating the unknown:

Phobias and fears

You may have heard that I am taking swimming lessons at the community centre. I am taking these lessons because of a little problem I had last summer. You all know that young children take baths quite often. Sometimes this is because their parents think they might be dirty, as if a little mud on the legs is something to be ashamed of. Sometimes, it is because their parents feel that a warm bath will cool them down, not that there is any logic in that reasoning at all. But anyway, one evening, I was very strongly invited to participate in a cooling-down session. At one point during my bath, though my mommy was watching me as she always does when I am in the tub, I wanted to prove that I hadn't quite cooled down yet, and I emptied my little pail of water right on the floor. My mommy must have thought I was in some kind of danger because she immediately pulled me out of the tub without asking my permission. This led to what I would describe as a medium temper tantrum on my part. Apparently, the cooling-down technique doesn't always work very well. My daddy came up to help and my mommy went to make a hot tea to cool off.

Later on, when my mommy had completely cooled off, she read me my bedtime story, sang my bedtime songs and told me she loved me, which is always nice to know, especially after an incident involving floors and water. Then she gave me to my teddy bear to keep me safe during the night, and she went down to have a moment's peace with my daddy. I heard my daddy say, "You know, you've got to wonder how it is that parents don't actually throw the baby out with the bathwater. The temptation is there!"

That evening, during that weird time when you are not awake anymore, but you are not asleep yet, my body had this idea that maybe my toes would go down the drain with the bathwater, and I would not be able to pull them back up, and I would be forever stuck in the bathtub, even though my parents are not the type to throw babies out with the bathwater. My teddy bear was probably already asleep because he didn't get involved at all. The next day, I completely forgot about this idea because I had a great time at daycare discussing fire trucks and heavy machinery with a new boy, who came equipped with a yellow tractor that produces very realistic noises. But when my daddy brought me upstairs for my bath, my whole body became attacked by the toes-down-the-drain idea. My stomach became trembly, and my legs and arms kind of hurt, and I didn't feel well at all. I started crying and saying that I would not go in the bathtub. My daddy tried all kinds of things to get me to go in, but I just couldn't, so finally he just washed me with a washcloth even though it had been a muddy day.

The following evening, the toes-down-the-drain idea came back, just as I was going up to prepare for bed, and again it attacked my body. So I cried over and over again and refused to go into the bathtub. My mommy is a very wise person, and she knows that things might be going on that she doesn't understand – this happens to her all the time, she says – so she was quite relaxed about it. Once again I submitted to the washcloth treatment.

This went on for several days, and it was becoming a problem for my parents because baths are very convenient in many ways. I must say it was a bit of a problem for me, too, because there are some toys I may use only in the bathtub. But the toes-down-the-drain idea kept attacking my body as soon as we even approached the bathroom. By then, my mommy and daddy had figured out that I was afraid of something – probably water, since water is the main ingredient in bathtubs. So they decided to sign me up for swimming lessons. The pool at the community centre is huge, at least eleventeen times the size of my bathtub, but I was not afraid of it at all because there is no drain in the pool. So the toes-down-the-drain idea stays home when we go to the pool.

Swimming lessons are a very interesting experience. They have great games and toys. I enjoy them quite a lot. I've made several friends at swimming lessons. We get to talk while we are all washed and dressed after class and we are waiting for our mommies to finish talking to the other mommies. I am discovering that other children's bodies can also be attacked by ideas. I think this is what Grandma would call a universal phenomenon.

Gregory is terribly afraid of the elevator in the community centre. The idea that attacks his body is that the doors will not open again and the lights will go out, and we all know that darkness is not very reassuring, even when the lights are on. I find this really strange because

I love elevators. My parents let me drive them whenever we meet one. They feel safe when I am at the controls.

Joshua is afraid of having his hair cut because of the plastic cape. The idea that attacks his body at the barbershop is that he is in an environment full of strangers with an awful lot of scissors lying around, and he can't get out of the plastic cape to defend himself if necessary. Joshua knows that scissors can be very dangerous things because of the time he got into his mother's sewing box. He didn't have to say more; we all knew what he meant. Who hasn't looked into their mother's sewing box? Again, Joshua's barbershop-cape idea is not an idea that would make my tummy tremble. I didn't say this to Joshua because I don't like to brag, but I feel fully confident when I go for a haircut. My mommy looks around the place with a big smile on her face as if to let everybody how she has the best-looking boy in the whole world. My mommy is so proud of me. Rightly so, I might add.

Grandma had a lot to say about being afraid. I suspect that she may have had, at some point in her life, an idea that attacked her body because she knows all there is to know on that subject. She explained that ideas attack little children's bodies quite often because little children are little. And because they are little, very often things are quite big in comparison, and there are many, many things that they don't understand. Little children and even bigger ones and even big people, who are called adults, and even very old people like Grandma, will try to make sense of what they don't understand. They make up stories to explain the mysteries of life. These stories are called ideas. Sometimes their ideas help them to be happy. Sometimes their ideas help them to be unhappy and afraid. The problem with ideas, or rather with the people who are having these ideas, is that people forget that there are many more ideas to be had. They think that their most recent idea will be their final one. And they forget to have new ideas.

A strange thing about afraid ideas is that a person's body is the first to know about it. When I have a trembly tummy and that pain in my arms and legs, it is because my body thinks that there is a danger. Grandma explained that this is what is called a fight-or-flight response. I don't know much about fights because I have not yet been given permission to fight, but I do know about flights because my mommy is an air traffic controller. When her friends come to visit, they tell the story about when Flight Eleventeen disappeared from the screen. It was not a good thing, apparently.

Grandma says it's generally not useful to try to make an idea go away, even an afraid idea. This would be insulting towards your own idea, and insulted ideas like to come back and fight for their right to be there. According to Grandma, it is better just to place your afraid idea among all kinds of other ideas. Then your afraid idea will not take up all the space inside you, and the other ideas may help your tummy to stop trembling. So Grandma helped me make up new ideas to put around the down-in-the-drain idea. My favourite one is that the drain will tickle my toes and make me laugh.

After this conversation we got back to Prince Igor, who had just been introduced to a giant crocodile that was very hungry. Immediately Prince Igor's tummy got a bit trembly, but he was able to invent lots of ideas to put around the crocodile idea. The idea that worked best is that he should just run away as fast as he could to the safety of the big cave. It is a well-known fact that crocodiles are afraid of the dark and also of ghosts, so Prince Igor knew that the crocodile would not come into the cave.

"Mommy, you say"

Mommy, you say,
There's a green ghost just outside
      the dining room window.

Child, I say,
Ghosts don't exist,
Therefore there cannot be green ghosts just outside
      the window.

Mommy, you say,
If that thing just outside the dining room window
Is not a green ghost, it is a big bad wolf.

Child, I say,
Most wolves are not bad,
And even if they were, they don't live around here.

Mommy, you say,
If that thing just outside the dining room window
Is neither a green ghost nor a big bad wolf,
It is most certainly a very scary furnace
Just like the one who lives in the dark in our basement,
And tries to come up at night.

Child, I say,
Furnaces can't climb stairs
And they serve a very useful purpose,
        especially during the winter.
They are not scary at all.

Mommy, you say,
How do you know all that?

Child, I say,
Because I am a mommy
And mommies are not scared at all of ghosts, wolves,
        furnaces or the dark.
Mommies are big and strong and brave
        and never afraid...

As long as their own mommy is around.

8

Going inside:

Time out

I must tell you about something that happened to Tyler last week. You may not believe this story, but it is absolutely true. Grandma says that the absolute truth is extremely rare, but this is one case where a story is absolutely true. I feel the need to relate the events exactly as they happened, in the name of every child who has been given a "time out." Time outs are not easy to deal with at the best of times, and there are no best times as far as time outs are concerned. You may think that this is a strong stand, but someone has to take it.

What happened is that Tyler was given a time out right in the middle of a birthday party. A birthday party, even if it is not mine, is supposed to be a happy event, and by definition, happy events preclude time outs. At least that is what Tyler thought, so he started to participate in the celebrations without worrying about a time out landing on him.

Well, he has learned one of life's hard lessons: there are no time outs for time outs.

My parents and I and several other big people and children were invited to Katrina's second birthday party. Katrina is four years old, but this is only her second birthday party because she was in the hospital when she turned one and also three. My mommy explained to me that birthday parties are allowed in hospitals, but Katrina didn't have one because she was too sick to blow out the candles on her cake. She didn't even have a cake, as she was too sick to eat anything. So this time, she was given an extra big birthday party, and everybody was very happy.

Katrina was born, as all children are at one point, but she was born with extra holes in her heart, whereas most children are born with the normal number of holes in their bodies. Extra holes in the heart will create serious problems for any child: mainly, blue skin. I have a book that explains about people who live in faraway lands, which is where Prince Igor is travelling in search of his teddy bear. It shows that children have skins of many colours, though each child is allowed only one skin colour throughout his or her life. My own skin is pink, except when I have a temper tantrum, in which case my skin turns red to indicate the strength of the explosion. I've noticed that nobody in the book on faraway lands has blue skin. Blue skin is reserved for children with holes in their heart. Blue skin is not something you want to have because then you have to go to the hospital, even if it's your birthday.

So the party was in full swing. That is an expression that means you are having as much fun as when your daddy pushes you really high on the swing in the park. Then came the time for the presents, and that's when Tyler got into trouble. Tyler has just turned two so there are many things he doesn't understand about life in general and parties in particular. He didn't understand that he should give the present he had brought for Katrina to Katrina. He wanted to keep it for himself. You have to understand that the present was not something he would have chosen for himself. He has no use for picture books with princesses with pink dresses and sparkling fingers who spend their time looking in mirrors to see if they can spot a frog. He prefers real-life stories like the one about Prince Igor. Sometimes I tell him about Prince Igor, but I must change the stories a bit because Tyler is afraid of crocodiles, deserts, some camels, and sheiks. Not giving the book to Katrina was Tyler's way of saying to everybody, "When I say something is MINE, I mean it."

Tyler, having just turned two, has only recently discovered the joys of kicking something – or, better still, somebody – when you are unhappy with life. So he tried his new kick on his mother's leg to make her understand he didn't want to give the book to Katrina. He had tried just saying, "No want," but generally parents don't accept "No want" when they are asking you to be nice. So although it was a birthday party, Tyler was picked up by his father and given a very long time out. Time outs are long by definition, but they are especially long when you have just turned two because you can't count. When your parents are counting your time out, they are trying to reassure you that they know what they are doing, but it's not that helpful if you don't know enough about counting to check that they are putting the numbers in the right order. For all you know, your parents might be stuck between two numbers till the party is over and you will have missed the cake and the balloons. Things can be very complicated when you have just turned two. I'm glad I'm past that stage.

Tyler finally was liberated from his time out thanks to the fact that his mother is an accountant and therefore she knows her numbers. But then he still had to hand over the present to Katrina. He decided to do so, but I could tell it wasn't because he had discovered the joys of sharing. It was because he now understood that time outs can be given to you even during a birthday party, and he didn't want to risk another one. Katrina was very nice about it; she even said Tyler could look at the pictures in the book.

I was somewhat surprised at Grandma's reaction when I told her this story. I expected her to oppose the use of time outs during a birthday party, since she is against all forms of torture. But it seems that the only thing she doesn't like about time outs is the fact that they are not properly named. She says that time outs should be called *time ins* because "going inside" is the whole purpose of a time out. She explained that a very important part of parents' work is to help their children develop a rich inner life, as this will turn out to be very useful when the children become big people. Big people who are autonomous, creative and generous often take time in to find out how they feel and think about things and how they want to act. It's called "leading your life from an inner authority." When you are a big person, you usually don't get time outs handed down to you if you are careful enough to give yourself enough time ins. But time outs *can* happen to you when you are a big person, even if you don't live with your parents, because what Grandma calls "society" will give you one if you don't behave well. Jails are a good example of time outs for big people. I wouldn't recommend jail because you would need someone to count to eleventeen zillion, and nobody can do that and you might be stuck in there forever.

Time outs can be quite frightening, even if they are given to you by people who know their numbers well. Whenever I receive a time out, my stomach becomes a little trembly, especially if I don't really understand why I have been given a time out. I'm pretty good at doing three or four things at the same time, any of which could attract a time out. Sometimes I don't know if I am timed out because I have refused to help put on my snowsuit, or because I have thrown my library book, or because I stepped on the box of my puzzle and sort of squished it. Even when my mommy or daddy tells me why I am being timed out, my tummy doesn't always understand.

Grandma says this is a normal reaction because at my age I must learn two things that don't always go together. First, I must learn that I am a separate being from my parents, and to do that I must experiment with saying "no" quite often and occasionally throwing my weight around. Second, I must also learn to listen to my parents because they are bigger and wiser than I am.

It's a normal reaction for a tummy to become a little trembly when you have to go in two directions at the same time. Everybody's tummy does that, even when you are a big person and don't even have a tummy anymore, just a stomach.

Grandma says that when I am in a time out, I can close my eyes and look at all kinds of pretty colours, or even think of the dog that is my friend (though nobody can see that dog except me). This helps a time out become a time in, and my tummy will like that. What also helps after a time out is that my mommy and daddy forget what I have done to get a time out, and they act like they love me as usual. Children whose parents have a short memory are very lucky.

Grandma says it would be nice if parents sometimes took time outs with their children. Parents need time ins, too, so they can look at the pretty colours inside of them or talk with their imaginary pets, but time ins are sometimes hard to find for parents because they don't have much time of any kind, either out or in. So parents could ask their children to share their time outs with them once in a while. It would help everybody's tummy.

"You are quietly working on the dinosaur puzzle"

You are quietly working on the dinosaur puzzle.

So far today, no time outs or moments in the corner.

I watch you playing so quietly

And tell you silently what I would never say out loud:

That every time you are sent to a time out,

I take a deep breath and send myself to a corner

     of my heart

where I dream of you.

After all, I say to myself,

This child and I have both contributed to this moment.

I deserve it, too.

So I dream faraway dreams:
I am sitting in my wheelchair in the Grand Hall
Applauding with all my might as you receive
        the Nobel Peace Prize.
I dream closer dreams:
Your new book, the definitive answer to the mystery
        of raising children,
Is launched today and you publicly thank
        your parents for their patience.
I dream still closer dreams:
You inscribe your college graduation picture
"Thanks for all your help and love"
And present it to me in a golden frame.
I dream even closer dreams:
The elementary school principal says,
"This child is so bright and has so much talent.
Thank you for choosing our school."

And still closer, I dream

That next year, six months into nursery school,

Your teacher says, "This is such a lovely child:

      polite, creative, yet disciplined,

Who enjoys sharing with the other children and likes

      vegetables for a snack."

So, dearest child, why are you so co-operative today?

I need my time in.

9

Learning the math of abundance:

Sharing

Now that I have told you about the time out Tyler got at Katrina's birthday party, I must tell you about sharing, since being told to share is what got him into trouble. Tyler is not the only child in the world who has gotten into trouble over the laws of sharing. I have not met one child who hasn't had at least a minor disagreement with his or her parents on that subject.

Tyler does not come to the library because he prefers toys to books, and we must respect this personal choice. But many other children attend the weekly gathering with the lady who reads to us and teaches us interesting songs. It's only when there are other people around you that you need to share, and this is when problems start, as they did last week at the library.

I must first explain that red is my favourite colour, and therefore I must make sure to obtain the red cushion for the reading circle. There are several red cushions, but only one that I really prefer, so I want the other children to know that it is mine. The way I do that is that I quickly go pick it up and bring it to my place in the circle. But once I have done that, a little problem starts developing, which is that I can't leave my place in case Cynthia decides she wants my red cushion. She, too, likes red, though I have tried to convince her that she likes yellow better. Cynthia is a new girl in the group, so she doesn't yet understand all the laws that I would like her to obey.

The library is a great big sharing place, as my mommy explained to me. They have eleventeen hundred books and movies that need to be shared by eleventeen zillion people, including many children. I am not yet completely fluent in numbers, so you will have to figure out for yourselves the quantity of sharing that needs to be done. What I am trying to say is that you might not get the cushion, the book or the movie that you want. And if you don't, you might not like that.

Before we go in the activity room, we gather in a room where there are many educational toys, and we get to play with them. An educational toy is a toy that would allow a library not to have to worry about broken windows. Most educational toys in a library are either too big to throw or they are affixed to the tables. When they do have pieces of a throwable size, you wouldn't be interested in throwing them. Foam rubber puzzle pieces do not travel well at all. It is in that room that there was quite a fuss the other day. I want to state right away that the fuss was not caused by me.

The fuss started when Ella, who was working on the fire engine puzzle, even though she is a girl, refused to let Jacob touch the puzzle pieces. Maybe Jacob was trying to help Ella because he thinks girls don't understand much about trucks. Maybe Jacob had been waiting for a long time for a chance to work on that puzzle. Maybe Jacob wanted to become friends with Ella. Maybe Jacob just wanted to get his mother's attention, since she was discussing toilet training with Thomas's mother and Jacob doesn't like his mother to discuss this subject, especially with Thomas's mother, since it seems that Thomas was toilet trained quite early. Nobody knows for sure what was going on in Jacob's head. And nobody knows for sure what was going on in Ella's head either. Maybe Ella was concentrating really hard on aligning the puzzle pieces, which is hard to do in a fire truck puzzle because of the ladders. Maybe Ella likes to work alone. Maybe Ella doesn't like Jacob and does not want to be friends with him. Maybe Ella didn't feel like sharing, since she has to share a lot at home because she has two brothers and altogether they have only one dog. Nobody knows for sure.

All we know is that she said "No" very loudly to Jacob, and when Jacob ignored her, she pushed him away. I'm quite certain that Jacob helped himself fall down on the floor because Ella had not pushed him that hard. Jacob started hollering, and everybody stopped talking and rushed to the scene. Rushing to the scene is an expression that means that when something interesting is happening, you run to see what's going on. Had I been in Jacob's slippers, I would not have hollered, as I don't like to waste a holler when a good shriek will do, but as Grandma says, all children are different and have different reactions to being insulted.

You might think that Ella's mommy would have told Jacob's mommy to tell Jacob to stop bothering Ella. And you might think that Jacob's mommy would have told Ella's mommy to tell Ella to share the puzzle with Jacob. But that is not at all how it went. On the contrary, Ella was told by her mommy to share the puzzle with Jacob because she has to learn to share. And Jacob was told by his mommy to leave Ella alone because he has to learn to ask politely rather than just grab the things he wants. Ella's mommy kept insisting that Jacob had the right to play with the puzzle, and Jacob's mommy kept insisting that Ella had gotten to the puzzle first and that Jacob must respect that. The two mommies kept on insisting, as insisting is part of a parent's job. Ella and Jacob were looking confused, as I would have been if all of a sudden it was my enemy's mommy who was on my side and my mommy was on my enemy's side. An enemy is somebody you don't like to play with because they get you into trouble. Prince Igor has met several enemies in his search for his teddy bear, but he has learned to try to transform them into friends because it's easier for him to go on with his travels if he does that. I don't have the time here to explain the techniques he has been using, but I'll describe them to you at another time if you are interested.

The strangest thing that happened is that Ella and Jacob moved quietly to a corner of the room where there are very interesting books and started looking at the same book as if they were best friends. Meanwhile, the mommies kept insisting and insisting. After a while we were told to go into the activity room, and Ella and Jacob came with us as if the whole fuss had never happened. Their mommies stayed in the back of the room talking quietly, each of them trying to be very nice to the other.

Grandma was quite excited when I told her this story because she likes to talk about the joys of sharing. Personally, I haven't yet met that many joys in sharing. I might even say that, so far, sharing has brought me more grief than joy. Grandma understands that it is difficult to learn to share, especially at my age since once again I seem to have to learn at the same time two things that don't seem to go together. I must learn that I am different from other people, and say, "This is me. This is you. This is mine. This is yours." At the same time, I must learn to say,

"This is mine, but I will share it with you." So by all standards, whatever standards are, sharing does not come naturally to children my age.

Apparently, sharing does not come naturally to humankind either, said Grandma. She proposed to examine the whole question from afar to help me understand. So Grandma explained to me that everything I can see, hear, feel, taste and smell has been invented by Life. Life is what makes things move, and Life needs to move to keep alive, so It created people, animals, plants and everything else. Grandma says that even rocks are alive, though I can't see it very well because rocks move very, very slowly. Personally, I think if you want to have a rock move, the easiest way is to throw it. However, the Life explanation might come in handy in case I ever throw a rock into my mommy's flowerbeds. I must remember it.

It seems that Life asks everything and everyone to move It, and in return for this small favour, It shares Its abundance. Abundance is all those books and movies that I can borrow from the library. Abundance is also the life, home, work and love that my parents share with me. Abundance is what I have when my Grandpa visits and sleeps in the room next to mine. During the night, if a bad dream jumps on me, all I have to do is yell, "GRANDPA!" and Grandpa pats my back till my teddy bear is ready to take over. Abundance is all over the place, says Grandma. When you open your eyes and your heart and recognize abundance, it becomes very easy to share because you realize that sharing does not take anything away from you. There is always more.

I must say at this point that I was quite surprised to learn from Grandma that people have been invented by Life. I have a book that Grandma gave me that explains how people were invented by big monkeys, and there are many pictures to prove it. This just goes to show that even when you are old you can still change your mind about things.

Grandma generally knows when enough is enough, so she stopped talking about how Life likes to move forward and offered to tell me more about Prince Igor. Prince Igor has just come to a new faraway land where everybody needs bright blue pebbles to exchange for food and toys. No problem – there were bright blue pebbles all over the place, several feet deep in some places, and people knew exactly how to find them. Well, just three days before Prince Igor's arrival, a bad person told everybody that the bright blue pebbles would soon disappear and that people would no longer have food and toys. So the people picked up all the bright blue pebbles and kept them for themselves, and now there is not a bright blue pebble in sight. Prince Igor is considering bypassing this faraway land, but he is not certain he should in case his teddy bear is there.

"Something
is making you
unhappy today"

Something is making you unhappy today.
Perhaps colic or the sniffles
Or even just adjusting to being alive.
Whatever it is, you are not enjoying
The good life that a three-month-old should enjoy.
A slow walk to the grocery store
Is what will do both of us good.

So I put you in your stroller

And start walking through the neighbourhood,

Hoping you will fall asleep.

You don't, but at least you become quiet.

We meet the old lady who lives on the corner.

She bends over to look at you

And you grace her with the most beautiful smile ever.

She seems to take your smile and tuck it

In some corner of her frail heart,

Storing it for when she will need a special blessing.

She whispers, "Thank you," and turns before I can see

    the tears.

You have been miserable all morning.

Colic and the sniffles can really ruin a day.

And yet from the very core of your being

You give the only thing that is yours to give.

I grab that special moment and put it in my heart,

For when I am very old and depending on others

To feed me, touch me and keep me warm.

I start walking again

And I say a prayer of thanks to you

For teaching me, way ahead of time,

To share even if I have nothing to give.

10

Taking care of your environment:

Toilet training

Grandma has been suggesting recently that I tell you everything I know about toilet training. As such, the subject of toilet training does not have the attraction for young children that it has for most adults, especially the parents of these young children. Though I have not been able to talk to all my friends to get their opinion on this subject, what I do hear from them is that toilet training is a highly overrated process, at least from the point of view of those who are being toilet trained. Most children I know could do without the hassle. However, Grandma thinks that there are many lessons to be learned, both for children and parents, in that process, and she would really like it if I could explain a few things to you on the matter. Grandma is not one to let the lessons of life go by without at least commenting on them, so I've agreed to broach the subject. The faster this gets done, the faster we will return to Prince Igor, who at this point is once more travelling in a desert, which is a place where toilet training, accomplished or not, would not be a problem, for obvious reasons.

My friends have agreed to share their toilet-training experiences and opinions with me on condition of anonymity. So, to make sure you do not recognize them, I shall change their names and the circumstances of their life. For example, Martin will not be called Martin, and he will not have the usual number of daddies, brothers and bedrooms. Also, since this is not a "true confession" type of report, I shall not let you know if I am toilet trained or not or somewhere in between. Toilet training is a private matter, and I wouldn't let you know that I was toilet trained even if I was, out of respect for my friends' feelings. You might think you can ask my parents if you desperately want to know, but as you don't know who my parents are – "Felix" being a pseudonym – you will have to do without that information. I'll have you notice that most people in the world don't have that information, and they still lead fulfilling lives.

A few of my friends have answered a little questionnaire I set up for research purposes. The first question is, "Who invented toilet training? And in what year?" The second question is, "If you could do without the hassle, would you?" And the third and final question is, "Are dinosaur stickers better than Smarties?" Claudia, who was the first to answer my questionnaire (this is not her real name and she may or may not be a girl), said that toilet training was invented by her mommy and that it was invented between the ages of two and three. Claudia said she could do without the hassle, but she can see the light at the end of the tunnel. The third question does not apply to Claudia because she has never been given a dinosaur sticker, since she may or may not be a girl.

Michael, who has three daddies, three brothers and three bed-rooms and therefore has three opinions on everything, says that toilet training was invented by a bad witch at Halloween; that so far he is succeeding in doing without the hassle; and that the best reward between dinosaur stickers and Smarties are Popsicles. Lara, who may or may not be a boy, says that toilet training was invented in the dark ages, as keeping dry during the night is something he is finding difficult. He doesn't know who invented the thing, but he is certain the inventor was not child-friendly. He could do without the hassle. As for dinosaur stickers versus Smarties, he is undecided, as it depends on the size of the stickers and the colours of the Smarties.

Well, there you have it. If you want to know how children feel about toilet training, just ask them. I cannot answer my own questionnaire, since I obviously know all the right answers, but I will tell you that toilet training has never been and never will be an issue at my house. My parents give me lots of freedom and respect my choices. As an example, my mommy always asks me which arm I want to put first in the sleeves of my snowsuit. My parents also issue lots of invitations: for instance, when they invite me to brush my teeth at bedtime. Invitations are nice. Children usually hate being told what to do.

Grandma was impressed by the research project I set up for the discussion on toilet training. Coming from her, this is quite a compliment because she always questions what research has been done before important political decisions are made. She expressed the opinion that toilet training can be quite a hassle for children and parents because it happens right when children are learning to say, "This is mine. This is not yours. I can say no if I want to and even if I don't want to." And also, "You can't make me," and for the first time the parents really can't! So parents have to be very creative to continue respecting their children's choices, while issuing strong invitations to enter a world where diaper bags can be devoted entirely to carrying favourite toys.

Grandma says that most big people are very well toilet trained, which is certainly a relief for all their creative and patient parents, but not all of these toilet-trained people have learned the *lessons* of toilet training. What are the lessons of toilet training?

First: Do not make a mess. And yet people throw their candy wrappers on the street, they drop cigarette butts on the ground, and some just pretend to pick up after their dog in the park.

Second: Get to know your body. Pay attention to its needs, its rhythms, its pain, its comfort. Learn to tell yourself and others what your body needs. And yet people ignore their bodies' needs. They push themselves too hard or not hard enough. They don't listen to warning signs of stress and illness.

Third: Say yes when you want to say yes. Say no when you want to say no. And know the difference. And yet people say no just to oppose authority and not because it's the right answer for them. And people say yes just because it is asked of them without checking if this is really what they want to say.

Fourth: Make mistakes as you must, because that is what humans do. Clean up after your mistakes. Don't beat yourself up because you have made a mistake. Learn to start over and be patient. Be grateful for the help you are given. And yet people dwell on their mistakes and become extremely self-critical. They want and need help, but they don't want to ask for it. They think they are supposed to find all the answers by themselves, and they deprive themselves of the joy of receiving help from their families, friends and co-workers. They forget that Life is a learning process, like toilet training is.

And *finally: Some things are private. Keep it that way.* No more needs to be said.

"Have all these people not been properly toilet trained?" asks Grandma.

I think Grandma needed to get a few lessons off her chest. Sometimes lessons weigh her down. It's good for her to let a few fly around the earth. I am sure she is grateful for the opportunity I have given her to do so. I like to help Grandma. It puts her in a good mood for telling long stories about Prince Igor's adventures.

"No, no, no, I tell you"

No, no, no, I tell you.

I won't do it.

I'm sick and tired of hearing your commands.

I'm sick and tired of being bossed around.

Everybody treats me like a child, especially you.

You are not my commander.

I have had it with having to obey.

I have had it with people telling me how I should live
      my life.

I'll tell you, and you had better listen,

I just can't stand your ordering me around.

Stop it this instant.

I don't want to have to repeat myself.

STOP THIS RIGHT AWAY!

So the next time you want the butter, dear husband,
Just remember that "Pass me the butter"
Won't get it to you.
In this house, the way to get butter is to say,
"Would you *please* pass me the butter, dear?"
And then I will understand that you finally
      understand
That I am not a two-year-old child.
And you will finally be able to eat your buttered toast,
Though by that time it may be cold buttered toast.

11

Defining reality:

Imaginary playmates

As you know, one of the advantages of being given a time out, or a time in, as Grandma calls it, is that it gives you time to visit old friends, such as the big dog that only I can see. The big dog's name is Pilfroy, and I have had the honour of choosing this name because Pilfroy is *my* dog. Pilfroy answers only to my command. He eats what I like to feed him, and he always says thank you, especially when I feed him chocolate cookies. He can go outside in the snow without boots, and he doesn't have to wear a coat, since he wears his fur all the time. He doesn't have to go to bed earlier than the other dogs. He can watch TV all day long if I decide the shows are educational. When we go in the car to visit Grandma and Grandpa, he comes with me and looks out the window to spot fire trucks and trains. I have to sneak him into the car because he won't ride in a car seat, and at our house, it's a very big rule that everybody has to ride in a car seat all the time. So he never says a word in the car.

One day, I told William, my friend at daycare, about Pilfroy. I can trust William totally. He would never tell on me, no matter what I do. William said that he also has a personal assistant who has become a friend, but his friend doesn't visit during time outs. He visits once William has been put to bed for the night, which is very helpful because William's daddy often has to go away on a plane. William's dog is actually a monkey, and his name is Banana. I think Banana is a fine name, and I considered for a moment changing Pilfroy's name to Banana, but right away Pilfroy appeared in person and growled to show that he didn't want to change his name.

Banana has been with William longer than Pilfroy has been with me, so William has many tales to tell about his monkey, and he told me this story. You know how it goes once your parents discover something about you that you haven't yet told them. They *talk* about it. Well, William's daddy overheard William and Banana conversing, and he said to William's mommy that their son had an imaginary monkey for a friend. William was very insulted, not because his daddy discovered Banana – William would have told him eventually – but because he said that Banana was imaginary. Imaginary means "not real," and Banana is very real. He even *talks* to William; can you be more real than that? So William and Banana discussed this situation, and Banana suggested a plan to make William's parents realize that Banana was real.

After spending the night perfecting the plan, William sent Banana to live in his bedroom closet. Banana didn't mind because that was part of the plan, and William had left plenty of healthy food and fresh air in a box for him. William's mommy came to wake him up and help him get dressed before breakfast. William acted as normally as he could, which probably made William's mommy immediately suspect that something was up. I'm not saying that William isn't normal, it's just that he likes to invent a new "rise and shine" routine every morning.

William's mommy served him his cereal. William really likes this cereal because it has raisins and warm milk in it, and he almost decided to put things off till the following day. But Banana appeared briefly and told William to go ahead with the plan – life in a closet doesn't have much appeal. So William refused to eat his cereal. When children don't want to eat, mothers inquire about tummy aches, then they touch your forehead and cheeks to check for fever, then they look at the clock, and then they sigh. And then they tell you to eat: don't you like that food anymore? William then looked his mommy straight in the eye and explained very calmly that he couldn't eat because Banana was not there to tell him to go ahead and eat. William has trouble with long sentences, as most children do till they are eleventeen, so it may have come out something like: "No want… Banana not here… Banana say not eat." William's mommy understood that William wanted a banana and offered him one. William refused. Finally, William's mommy said he could have breakfast later. She packed a big snack, since they were going shopping for a new snowsuit. William refused to put on his snowsuit and once again explained that he couldn't do it because Banana had not told him to. Once more there was a bit of confusion because William's mommy again thought he wanted a banana. I will say here that I am glad that my dog is called Pilfroy. There is no possibility of confusion. Of course, after a while William did get to be dressed in his snowsuit, mittens and all, because you can't refuse a snowsuit forever without provoking a time out. But then William wouldn't let his mommy put him in the car seat. Well you get the picture, and the picture was not a pretty one.

This went on and on all morning, and the shopping was not made easier by all this, but finally William's mommy caught on and said to William, "Why don't we bring Banana along with us?" This was very brave on the part of William's mommy because she had no idea what Banana was or how taking in a monkey would affect their lives in the long run. Banana let himself out of the closet, having eaten all the chocolate cookies and breathed every inch of the fresh air, and joined William and his mommy at the shopping centre. That evening, William's mommy brought an extra chair to the dinner table and also put an extra place setting to make William's daddy understand that Banana was real. William's daddy understood right away because he works in a furniture store.

Grandma liked this story because she greatly admires people who have imaginary friends. She says that imagination is a gift that Life gives to people to thank them for spreading Life. She has noticed that people who are recognized as great "Life spreaders" have a great imagination, and they use it all the time. They see things in unusual ways, they cherish their dreams, they make up new ideas for themselves when the old ones are not helpful anymore, they wonder how they can help others, they like to solve problems. These people don't try to solve the mystery of Life, which would be very insulting to Life; they learn to contemplate it. According to Grandma, you can't have enough imagination. The capacity to imagine is never bad. It's what you do with your images that makes the difference between good and bad. This is true for many things, such as feelings and thoughts.

Grandma thinks that all people are born with a huge capacity for imagining their lives, but something happens too often between childhood and bigpeoplehood that makes people believe that "imaginary" is the opposite of "real," and that they have to choose one or the other, meaning of course that they have to choose "real." Having to choose between "imaginary" and "real" is a very sad thing because "imaginary" and "real" are made to work together and should never be separated in Life.

Grandma added another thought that really surprised me. She said that big people as well as children can have imaginary playmates. Grandma told me that when she has made a big mistake and feels bad about that, she imagines that there is someone inside of her who really likes her and says nice things to her even though she has made a big mistake. She says that helps her find the courage to say she's sorry and try to repair the mistake. Grandma knows people who will imagine that there is a bad person inside of them, like a bad witch who says nasty things. This bad witch scolds the people when they have made a mistake, and as a result the people feel worse than they did before. It then becomes harder for these people to say they're sorry and fix their mistake. It's hard to explain why a person would imagine such a witch. Grandma has often tried to help people imagine nicer people inside of them.

Grandma sometimes can go on and on about things such as imaginary playmates or witches, but I don't mind it because I have Pilfroy with whom I can discuss things if I need some relief from big words. But I did ask Grandma if she imagined *me*, as I am quite real, or so I think. I don't mind *having* an imaginary friend, but I wouldn't want to *be* one. Grandma replied that of course she imagines me all the time, and so do my mommy and daddy. For instance, when I am grumpy, my parents imagine me as having a trembly tummy or a fever or being hungry or tired or hug deprived. To be able to imagine me well, they observe me closely, talk to me, ask questions and touch me. Most of the time, I must admit they are very good in their imaginings. The only thing they have trouble with in that area is imagining that I may be chocolate-cookie deprived.

"I watch you play with your little friends"

I watch you play with your little friends
Or perhaps I should say your little enemies,
Observing the way you treat them
And the way they treat you back.
I can't figure this out.
You are such a gentle and easygoing child.
Shoving and kicking and threatening to bite:
This is just not you.
But then, maybe it is?

One day, you are the nicest child ever
And I brag about you to everyone who will listen.
The next day, you are the worst child ever
And I make sure I tell no one about you.
But then I wonder:
Have you really changed that much in a day?
Or is it I who is making you up?

Trying to figure you out
Has become a lifelong goal.
I keep an eye on you at all times.
I really, really want to know who and what you are.
But the minute I think that I have you down pat
I realize that I don't and I'm back to square one.
You sure are keeping me on my toes!

So, dearest child, dearest angel, dearest devil,

I have a very simple request,

One that you can easily grant me

If you are the angel I think you to be

And, alas, one that you can easily deny me

If you are the devil I also think you to be:

Will the real you please stand up

So I can finally sit down?

12

Finding our limitations:

Burnout

Alicia is a very nice girl who comes to the library often. I like her quite a bit, as she understands that at least one of the red cushions should be reserved for me. She even saved one for me last week, as we were a bit late due to a snowsuit incident that had occurred at home. Alicia brings her grandmother to the library. Her grandmother wears glasses, so of course she is interested in anything that has to do with books. Alicia also has a mommy, but her mommy hasn't been feeling well recently so she has to sleep a lot, which is why Alicia's grandmother has the privilege of taking care of Alicia and her big sister, Meghan.

Alicia knows that I am a good listener. Being a good listener comes naturally when you are little and don't yet know all the words you need to talk. Children must listen to their parents all day long, which may have its drawbacks, but it does develop good listening skills, or at least this is the official explanation. So Alicia told me how her mommy became not well. It started on grocery shopping day. Alicia always used to go grocery shopping with her mommy, and they had established a nice routine. Alicia would sit in the grocery cart and make suggestions to her mommy about good food. When they passed the candy aisle, Alicia would point at the chocolate candy, and her mommy would say: "When we get home, I will give you a nice little snack of grapes and cheese." And then Alicia would pretend she was disappointed. Then Alicia and her mommy would line up to pay for the groceries so they could take them home. On grocery day, the family would eat spaghetti for dinner. Alicia really likes spaghetti, as her mommy understands that you can't eat spaghetti without some mess. I hear that girls, more than boys, must try to always be clean and avoid messes. I must get Grandma's opinion on this.

Well, that particular day, Alicia and her mommy put a huge amount of food in the cart because there was company coming for the weekend and Alicia's mommy and daddy would prepare lots of special meals. Alicia and her mommy were walking through the store to line up for the money part when all of a sudden Alicia's mommy picked Alicia up out of the cart and carried her out of the store, leaving the cart and all the food behind. Alicia didn't understand what was going on, especially when her mommy sat down in the car and started to cry and say over and over again: "I just can't go on. What's happening to me?" Alicia started to cry, too, because a crying mommy can be somewhat frightening, so then her mommy finished putting Alicia in her car seat, and said, "I love you, honey," and blew both their noses and drove home.

It was really strange when they got home because once again Alicia's mommy started to cry, this time probably because she had forgotten where the groceries were. Alicia tried to tell her where they were, but her mommy kept on crying. Then Alicia's big sister, Meghan, came home from school, and she asked their mommy why she was crying. Their mommy said she was just tired and please go and watch TV for a while if they wanted to help.

So Alicia and Meghan decided to help, but their favourite show did not seem as funny as it usually did. They turned the TV up loud to make it funnier, but that doesn't work too well when your mommy is crying in the kitchen. And also, a trembly tummy makes more noise than the TV, to the point that you can hardly hear. This is what Alicia discovered that day. When Alicia's daddy came home from work, he was surprised to see that the spaghetti dinner was not ready. Actually, Alicia and Meghan had already had their dinner, their mommy having served them the exact same cereal that they had eaten for breakfast that morning.

Of course, Alicia's daddy asked what was going on. All Alicia's mommy could answer was that she didn't even know if she liked spaghetti. They had been eating spaghetti every Thursday night forever, but she didn't know if she liked spaghetti at all, and not knowing that is what made her cry. It turned out that there were many other things that Alicia's mommy didn't know: what was happening to her, where she was going with her life, what would become of the girls if she got sick, what would become of the house if she stopped working, what people were going to say, and many other things that Alicia and Meghan didn't really understand. Alicia's mommy kept crying and crying, even though their daddy talked to her in a very nice way. Finally, she said goodnight to the girls and went to bed.

Alicia's daddy made himself some eggs and toast, though he had eaten eggs and toast that very morning, and took the food to the family room to be with the girls. I am beginning to think that eating exactly the same thing for dinner that you've eaten in the morning is a sure sign that something is not going very well. Eating chocolate cookies and milk might be a better thing to do than repeating your breakfast. My mommy says that chocolate cookies may not be good for your health, but they are very good for your heart. Alicia's daddy explained that their mommy was not feeling well, but they were not to worry; he would take care of them. All they had to do was continue being good little girls and everything would be all right. But then he called their grandmother and said that he was worried about what was happening to Alicia's mommy, and that he couldn't understand what was going on.

The following day, Meghan went to school and Alicia to daycare, and their mommy went to see a doctor, though she seemed to have trouble even getting out of bed. From what Alicia understood later, the doctor listened to their mommy's heart and said that her heart and her head were very tired and that she needed to stop working and rest for a long while. And the doctor said that Alicia's mommy was crying a lot because it was a way for her body to tell her things. Alicia's mommy hadn't been listening to her body enough and now was a good time to cry if necessary. Well, that evening, Alicia's mommy continued crying a lot. Her body must really have been telling her things.

What happened afterwards is that Alicia's grandmother started coming quite often to help out. That grandmother belongs to Alicia's daddy. The other grandmother, the one who belongs to Alicia's mommy, was not invited to come and help. Alicia's mommy said to their daddy, "I don't want my mother around me at this time. I respect her and I love her, but she is the one who taught me that I had to always be strong and do things perfectly all the time. She would probably push me to use willpower to pick myself up and get back into things. Being with her would just bring back memories of the good little girl that I was supposed to be all the time, always helping around the house, always smiling, while my brothers were out there having all the fun. I don't always agree with *your* mother – sometimes she annoys me no end – but at least she's not part of my childhood. And she doesn't seem to try to be all things to all people. I even envy her sometimes." So that's how Alicia got to see a lot more of her grandmother.

Well, that is quite a scary story, if you want my opinion, except for the grandmother-coming-to-visit-more-often part, which is a nice part. Grandmothers certainly are helpful when you have a trembly tummy. Grandma was very interested, as she likes stories where people are learning things about themselves. That is probably why Prince Igor is forever learning something in his travels. Last week, he learned that giant tigers can be dangerous to your health, even if their stripes might trick you into thinking they are not aggressive. Grandma says that many families today don't seem to have enough time to do and be all the things that are needed to be a healthy family. According to Grandma, it's useless just to tell the people in the family to take more time for themselves. That doesn't work because if you don't have time, how can you take more? It's like saying to take a chocolate cookie when there are no chocolate cookies around.

But what people do have are *moments*. People may and should take many moments because, unlike *time*, moments are all over the place and can be had just for the taking. A moment apparently has the same good effect that chocolate cookies have, and you're not stuck with a sugar high. My mommy stores the sugar up high in the cupboard because she doesn't use it often. She says a sugar high will make you feel low. People need to take many moments during their day because moments help them deal with time. It's good for people to take moments for themselves and also to exchange moments with others because moments need to circulate to have a positive effect. An example of a good moment is when you say "thank you" to someone in your family. This type of moment is good because it says, "I have seen you," and being seen in the right way feeds your heart. Another type of moment is when you breathe really slowly and deeply to tell your body that you appreciate what it's doing for you. Another type of moment is when you look around you to see what you haven't seen yet – for example, the light in the big maple tree by our house. There are many other types of moments, and each person gets to know what their favourite ones are. The important thing to remember is that taking many moments is what builds our strength to be able to deal with time.

I seized the moment, and Grandma and I joined Prince Igor in his travels. At this point, Prince Igor was taking in the sunset, but he was also keeping an eye on a noise that indicated the presence of an unfriendly tiger.

"Everything was going so well"

Everything was going so well.

The children, all bright and healthy and enjoying
home schooling.

The husband, strong, hardworking and good looking.

The garden, definitely the most luscious in
the neighbourhood.

The house, up to the best standards of orderliness
and cleanliness.

The five committees, all working smoothly under
my direction.

The church choir, well directed and harmonious

To lift my spirit and perhaps redeem my soul.

And then one day, suddenly, a crack in this perfect life.
And then another crack and yet another and another.
I fell right to the bottom of an abyss and found
      I couldn't move.

Within a very short while, the voice started whispering,
"Pull yourself together, dear, I know you can do it."
The whisper became louder and turned into
      a strong command:
"Pull yourself together, dear. Now."
The whispering kept me from sleeping
But the command went unheeded. I just couldn't move!

Finally, I dragged the voice and myself to consult
      a wise person.
"The Voice," said the wise person, "speaks in the name
      of all the other voices

who have a strong opinion on how you should live
        your life.
I'll help you pull yourself together
But you must pull together only what is really you.
The bottom of an abyss is a great place
To listen and look quietly around you.
Listen to the voices and decide which are really yours."

Air all the bedding once a week?
The voice of Great Aunt Bertha, who lived in a very
        humid climate.
The library committee?
The voice of my father, who established a library
        in our small village.
Home schooling?
The voice of my mother, for whom education
        was so important.

All those voices, and so many more of them

        not really mine.

I decided to rearrange my inner choir.

I fired quite a few bad singers

And kept only the ones who would follow my direction.

And under my direction, the church choir,

The one that other people can hear,

Has never sounded so beautiful.

Now that I've pulled only myself together.

13

Leaving home:

Daycare

One day last week, when I arrived at my daycare house, I quickly noticed that there was a new boy. His name is Nathan, and he has black hair. He had brought a fire engine with him. I have seen several boys with that kind of black hair in my life, but I had never seen a fire truck with such a long ladder and so many wheels. Of course, I was quite interested in making friends with Nathan as soon as possible. Denise, our caregiver, made us say Nathan's name aloud and also say welcome. "Welcome" is what you say when somebody thanks you (I already knew that, of course), but I learned that it also can mean that you can come into my house and I will share some of my toys with you for a while.

Nathan's daddy was also there, and Denise made us say hello to him. Nathan had wrapped his arms around his daddy's leg, and he looked determined to stay in that position because every time Denise asked him to come and play with us, he also wrapped his head around his daddy's leg. I thought this might be a good chance to let Nathan share his fire truck with me, since he wasn't using it right at that moment. But when I picked up the truck to start going to a fire, Nathan let out such a big holler that I immediately understood that I wouldn't be a firefighter that morning. So I went to build a house with the wooden blocks, and I even let Zoë put her doll in my house to show Nathan that I could be a reliable friend.

That morning, Nathan and his daddy stayed only till snack time. They left because Nathan's daddy was getting a sore leg and also because Nathan had not yet decided that he wanted to belong to our group. The next day, he came back, and this time he brought with him a yellow airplane that is an ambulance. An ambulance is a car with beds in it, and if you are not feeling well, you can go and lie down in one of the beds and the driver of the ambulance will go really fast all around the block to help you feel better. Some ambulances are airplanes, and that is for when you need to travel long distances to become better. Airplanes go faster than cars because there are no red lights in the sky. As soon as I saw the airplane ambulance, I knew for sure that I wanted to be friends with Nathan. The sad thing that day is that Nathan did not understand that I wanted to be friends with him. He only wanted to be friends with his daddy, and when his daddy left, he cried a lot. His daddy was also very sad. I know because I looked through the window when he went outside, and I could see that he was crying, too.

My tummy became a little trembly when Nathan cried, and I wanted my mommy to come pick me up as soon as possible, though it wasn't even morning snack time. Denise decided that we all needed a bit of help to feel happy, so she asked us to help make dessert. We worked on a recipe that involved chocolate pudding, crumbled chocolate cookies and gummy worms. I was given the most important job, which was crumbling the cookies. It was really messy, but Denise knows that a good mess can help bring back your happiness. So we were a lot happier after that work, and even Nathan forgot several times that he was totally miserable. What helped Nathan become happier, also, is that Denise smells really nice and her hands are warm. No child would want to be in daycare with someone whose smell they don't like or who has cold hands. It would be like being in daycare with a bad witch.

Denise explained to us that day that Nathan came from a faraway land. As you know, I am very interested in far away lands because that is where Prince Igor is travelling. I thought for a while that Nathan might have met Prince Igor before he came to live with us in a closer land, but Nathan hadn't. I was a little disappointed, even though I know that Prince Igor belongs to a story. I think that if I can see Prince Igor, maybe other children can, too. In Nathan's faraway land, they don't have snow, only lots of fruit that grow on big trees, but Nathan didn't have to eat the fruits if he didn't like them. In that faraway land, the mommies don't wear the same clothes that my mommy does. I know because Nathan's daddy showed Denise some pictures of Nathan when he was a baby, and many mommies were in the pictures. Denise showed us these pictures because she likes people who do things differently from us. She says that we can learn a lot from people who don't do things like we do.

Nathan doesn't cry now when his daddy leaves him in the morning, though he looks like he might cry any moment. His lips are a little bit trembly, and he holds on to Denise's hand when the door closes. I always watch his daddy through the window because Nathan is busy not crying. His daddy's face doesn't cry anymore either, but he sits in his car for a little while because he needs to blow his nose out. I think that when he cries, the water comes out through his nose rather than through his eyes.

Grandma was keen to learn that we had a new friend at daycare. Just like Denise, she likes people who come from faraway lands because they don't do things exactly as we do in the closer land. She thinks that Nathan and I can become very good friends because good friends are usually quite different from each other, and that's what makes them good friends, except for when they fight. I haven't started to fight with Nathan. This may be because we are not good enough friends yet. Also, I think my mommy is waiting a while before giving me permission to fight because she has other permissions to give me first.

I also wanted Grandma to explain why Nathan's daddy sort of cries when he leaves him at Denise's house. After all, he is not the one who's being left with total strangers. And he doesn't have to obey all the rules and at least taste everything that we are served for lunch. Well, Grandma said that she didn't know for sure why Nathan's daddy sort of cries because the only sure way to know would be to ask him. However, Grandma did have a couple of ideas on that subject. An idea is like a picture that you have when you turn your eyes to the inside of your head. According to Grandma, it is a great idea to have many ideas.

Grandma explained that mommies and even daddies sometimes have trembly tummies, maybe even more often than little children, and that may make them sort of cry. Parents have to do two very important things with their children, and sometimes these two very important things make them feel that they have to go in two different directions. As I may have mentioned earlier, going in two different directions will make the strongest of tummies tremble, at least for a little while. The first important thing that parents do is bring their children into the world. That means that they make a baby be born. The parents are really glad to have the new baby, and they want to make sure the baby will always be safe and happy. So they need to keep the baby and protect him or her for a long, long while, and they like that because they love their baby. The other important thing that parents have to do is to help prepare the baby to leave home one day and find his or her own place in the world. Well, that's hard for parents because they will always feel that their baby is too little to leave home, even when the baby is grown and completely toilet trained, including during the night. And even when the baby becomes a really big person who is old enough to become a babysitter. Sometimes the parents will feel sad when they think that their baby will grow up to belong to the whole world, though that is what is good for the baby. And that can make any mommy or daddy cry, that's for sure. When Nathan's daddy leaves him at daycare, he probably realizes that Nathan is old enough to be without him for at least a little while, and that the little whiles will turn into long, long whiles even more as Nathan grows.

Another idea that Grandma had about Nathan's daddy is that he and Nathan have come from a faraway land, and maybe he misses his friends and his own grandma. He will miss Nathan while he is at Denise's, and maybe he is really tired of missing people. I can understand that because one day my mommy went away for two sleeps, and my tummy was trembly and my throat hurt when my daddy was putting me to bed. When my mommy came back, I was really glad to see her and I told her never to go away again, and I cried a little bit. One of the reasons Prince Igor has left home is because his teddy bear misses him greatly, and he must find him as soon as possible. But my mommy hasn't lost her teddy bear, so she has no reason to go away. Speaking of Prince Igor, in case you are worried, let me reassure you that Prince Igor *will* find his teddy bear. At this very moment, he is travelling in Nathan's faraway land in case the bad people have hidden his teddy bear in a fruit tree.

"such a long time ago..."

such a long time ago...

I watch you sleep, my son.

You are so tiny

As day-old babies are, of course.

Your mother is resting upstairs.

After all, she has put in a hard day's work.

And I ponder the question for the first time in my life.

I take you from your cradle

And bring you to the kitchen

Where your grandmother is cooking loads of food.

And I ask the question

That a son can ask only his mother.

"How soon is it safe to leave the baby
By himself in his room?"
Your grandmother smiles.
She found the answer to that question a long time ago.
"For now, a few minutes at a time."

I want to know more. Now.
I met this baby only a few hours ago
And already I know that he'll never be out of my heart.
But how will I know when he is ready to be out of my sight?
How will I know that this little guy is ready
To leave to go to all the schools of life,
From kindergarden to university?
How will I know that he is ready
To go to his life?
Your grandmother smiles again, saying,
"Your child will tell you."

And now...

We are sitting in the living room
watching your tiny baby sleep
while your wife is resting after all that hard labour.
Our hearts are full of joy
And we gently talk about your mother,
who so much would have loved to meet this child.
And suddenly you ask the question
That a son can ask only his father:
"How soon is it safe to leave the baby
By himself in his room?"

14

Talking without words:

Gymnastics

I don't know if you know what gymnastics is. I am asking because not everybody knows. I do now, but when I was a baby, I had no idea that gymnastics existed. I'm sure you want to know all about it because it is so much fun you wouldn't want to go through life without it.

Gymnastics is in a big, big room that is full of really interesting and fun things. First of all, you get to take your shoes off, and then you can climb over all kinds of big beds and barrels, and there are ladders and slides and big circles that you can hang on to and fly way up high into the air. Most of my friends and I are not allowed to jump on the couch in our houses. I'm not allowed because my parents do not consider jumping up and down on the couch an educational activity. But at gymnastics, everybody can jump up and down on the jumpolines. There is even a nice lady who really likes children, and she shows us how to jump even higher and throw a ball at the same time. Jumping up and down on things will often get children into deep trouble, especially when there is also some throwing that involves a flower vase. At gymnastics, however, that behaviour is considered good for your health, and the nice lady will even give you a sticker to thank you for behaving so well. And there are no flower vases to complicate your life.

So it is hard to get into trouble at gymnastics, but my friend Maxwell was able to manage it last week. Maxwell is what Grandma calls a free spirit. Prince Igor was once visited by a Spirit during the night who gave him a clue to where his teddy bear was hidden. I can't remember if that particular Spirit was free or if you had to give him pennies. I think a free spirit is someone who is very good at disappearing and reappearing in unexpected places because that's what Maxwell does. If Maxwell can find a place to hide, he'll go for it. At gymnastics, there are a lot of places to hide in, since the beds and barrels and blocks are very, very big. That is what makes gymnastics so interesting.

That morning, Maxwell kept running away from his group, and his mommy had to run after him to bring him back so he could do the games as we were told. At one point, his mommy was telling another mommy that Maxwell is always running away and hiding and that she's at her wits' end, and right then, Maxwell made his getaway and disappeared. After a few moments, everybody started looking for him and calling his name. Some people checked the door in case he had escaped outside. All of a sudden, this huge black-and-red shriek came from the cupboard under the stairs we take to go up to the jumpolines. The shriek went right up to the ceiling and covered the whole gymnastics room, it was so big. I immediately thought that Maxwell had encountered a Cupboard Ghost, and I know from personal experience that these ghosts can be extremely frightening. All the mommies probably thought that Maxwell had cut himself on something in the cupboard or found some poison. Mommies tend to think of blood or poison when their children are out of their sight. They all put their hand on their hearts and cried "Oh, my God!" and rushed to the cupboard. And out came Maxwell with a big grin on his face. The big grin lasted a very short time because Maxwell's mommy started to do some yelling of her own, and a mommy's yelling will wipe the grin off the face of the freest of spirits.

I don't know if you know the difference between a shriek and a holler. A shriek is a holler in the shape of an arrow. I prefer a holler to a shriek; it's less tiring for the throat. Also, even though a shriek will travel higher and faster than a holler, I find that a holler takes better care of a trembly tummy. But, as Grandma likes to say, to each his own, so if shrieking is Maxwell's thing, who am I to say he should choose differently? At my house, neither hollering nor shrieking are considered acceptable behaviour. My parents have explained that their hearing is perfect, and there is no need to take that tone of voice.

We all got back to having fun at gymnastics, except for Maxwell, who was taken into the office by his mommy, who had stopped yelling but apparently still needed to get some words out of her system and put them into Maxwell's. Maxwell joined us after a few minutes and continued having fun at gymnastics because that's what we were all there for, but I could tell there were a lot of his mommy's words in his system. He couldn't jump as high as usual, and he didn't even ask to go into the big pit with the foam rubber blocks.

Grandma liked this story because she likes free spirits. I think she might have been one herself when she was my age. Grandma may have been a person detective before I was born because she is always very interested in trying to find clues about children. A clue, in case you have never heard that word, is like a little arrow that shows you something you are looking for that you know is there but you can't see it. At Easter, I had trouble finding one of my Easter eggs, so my daddy sort of made an arrow with his fingers to show me that the egg was hidden under the sofa. When I found the egg, I also found my blue train engine and the puzzle piece with the lion's head on it. Grandma says that when you find something about a person, you often find other things that you thought were lost, and that makes you happy. So it's usually worth your while to spend some time figuring out why children are doing what they are doing. You might find something that makes you happy, or at least helps a trembly tummy, if you have one.

According to Grandma, it's very easy to see what people are doing. You just have to open your eyes for that. What you don't see as easily is *why* the people are doing what they are doing. For that, you have to open your heart and your brain, which is different from opening just your eyes. I could see with my eyes that Maxwell was hiding in a cupboard that possibly contained a Cupboard Ghost. What I could not see, unless I opened my heart and my brain, is *what* made Maxwell want to hide, right in the middle of gymnastics, right in the middle of a conversation his mommy was having with another mommy, and *what* makes Maxwell want to hide often. When you do something often, it is called a habit. Why had Maxwell taken up this habit? He must certainly understand by now that his parents don't approve of it. Why does he keep doing it? This is quite a mystery.

Grandma explained that one way to try to solve that mystery is to think that Maxwell, when he hides, is trying to do something that will help him. We don't know what Maxwell needs help with, and maybe Maxwell himself doesn't know. But we may decide to think that he is hiding because some good will come out of it somehow. For example, he may want to check that his mommy will always come looking for him.

Everybody knows that his mommy would, of course, come looking for him – I know that and I've never even set foot in Maxwell's house. But maybe *Maxwell* is not so sure about it. He has no "real" reason to think that his mommy would not look for him, but he has his own reasons, and to him they are as real as anybody else's, so he acts accordingly. His intentions, though he might not be able to say what they are, are good. Of course, we must admit that the *method* he has chosen to reassure himself has become an annoying habit for everyone around him. But if you make Maxwell stop using his method without wondering about his intentions, he'll probably just invent another method to reassure himself, and his new method might not be nicer than the first one. We must remember that Maxwell is a free spirit. Free spirits, according to Grandma, tend to go on inventing new things. Maxwell can very well go on inventing new methods till he is finally reassured that though his mommy brought him a baby sister which he never even asked for, his mommy will always come looking for him.

Grandma and I got back to Prince Igor, who is still travelling in the faraway lands in search of his teddy bear. Prince Igor has made many friends while travelling, but at this point, one of his friends, the one who plays the magic flute, has picked up a very bad habit. Every time Prince Igor and his friends and his camels are hiding from the bad people, this friend brings out his flute and plays a few notes. Of course, the bad people hear this and rush to the hiding place, and everybody has to run away and find a new hiding place. But the magic flute player friend insists that his flute could put all the bad people to sleep, once he has learned to play a proper lullaby. That might be a good idea, according to Prince Igor, but there is a problem: the magic flute player never practises to play a lullaby – all he likes to practise is dance music. It's going to be hard work to find the good intentions tonight, I can tell.

To finally be free to move in unconfined spaces.
Much too young to do it, you rolled off a bed
And I caught you just in time.
Much too young to do it, you crawled,
But only for a short while,
As you then proceeded to walking
And from there quickly went on to running.
And I was always behind you
To catch you just in time.

Then you started vaulting over your toys
And discovered the joys of jumping.
"Look, mommy, I'm on the jumpoline!"
And I was right next to the couch
Ready to catch you just in time.

From then on, you climbed, stretched,
Twisted, spun, gyrated, bounced,
Plunged, leapt, sprung, hopped, skipped,
Everywhere and every moment you could
And I was always as close as I could be
To catch you just in time.

But, my dearest, my darling, my sweet child,
This has gone far enough.
Now that you are 21
And have signed up for that course in aerial acrobatics
I do want you to clearly understand
That if ever you fall out of the sky
I won't be able to catch you just in time.
This time, "The sky really is the limit."

15

Going beyond appearances:

The child with a disability

The other day, it was Mother's Day. You may have heard about Mother's Day. In case you haven't, it's a day when all the children have the opportunity to learn to say "thank you" to their mommies and appreciate what they do for you, even if it is serving you broccoli. Also, it's a day when you can go pick flowers for your mommy from any garden in your street and nobody will make you say "I'm sorry" to a neighbour you don't even know. All the other days, you could get into big trouble for doing that. Mind you, this kind of trouble has never happened to me, as I am too young to go outside the house without my mommy or daddy to watch me. But Martin, my friend who has two daddies, two houses and two brothers but only one dog, has had this happen to him, and he told me all about it.

On Mother's Day, I helped my daddy make pancakes for mommy for breakfast. I got to break two eggs in a big bowl, and the other egg – the one we didn't need – slipped onto the floor by accident. Since we have no dog that likes to lick food off the floor, we had to pick up the egg by ourselves and wash the floor, and that was great fun. More and more I am allowed to help clean up the messes I make. Cleaning up the messes is nice because it gives you some extra time to enjoy them, and it doesn't prevent you from making new messes another time. So don't worry about it if your parents want you to be involved in the cleaning up.

After breakfast, we got all dressed up in nice clothes, and we went to visit a family who has two children and one mommy and one daddy. The mommy's name is Madeleine. I'm sorry, I don't remember the daddy's name. We went to celebrate Mother's Day with them because Sebastian's mommy is a very special mommy, according to my mommy, and my mommy knows all about mommies. The reason Sebastian's mommy is a special mommy is that Sebastian is a very special child. His sister is called Anna. She is much older, maybe nine or eleventen, and she is not as special, but I like her anyway because she always listens to me, even when I don't talk. Sebastian is older than I am, but he's not bigger than I am. That is because his bones don't grow well at all, even though his mommy has fed him lots of good vegetables. His face is funny looking because his eyes are not completely open. He's allowed to stick his tongue out anytime he wants, even in front of people. Mommy told me that his heart has a hole in it, and sometimes he has to go to the hospital because his ears get sick too. Sebastian loves me, I can tell, because he gives me big hugs.

When we got to Sebastian's house, we all said "Happy Mother's Day" to each other because that is what everybody is supposed to say. You can even say it to somebody who's not a mommy and everybody will just laugh. We ate some very good sandwiches and there was a cake. There were letters written on the cake and also a big yellow sun. I can't read yet, except in my own storybooks, so I didn't understand what the letters meant, but that's not important in the case of chocolate letters. Your tummy likes them anyway. Sebastian's mommy then said, "Today is Mother's Day, and everybody remembers to say thank you to the mothers. But I want to remind everybody that if there are mothers, it is because there are children. Having children is an immense privilege. Children invite their parents to grow all the time and travel inside to places they never even knew existed. For this I am immensely thankful."

All the big people clapped their hands to show they liked what Sebastian's mommy had said. And then Sebastian's mommy started to cry a little, and she said, "When Sebastian came along, I was really discouraged. I felt that Sebastian did not have what he needed to live a fulfilling life, and that I was unable to help him live as fully as he could. For months and even years, I felt that our family had been hit by very bad luck and that we would never know real happiness again. I want to tell you that this has changed."

Then Sebastian's mommy pointed to the cake. There was less sun on the cake, as Sebastian had been poking his finger in the icing and licking it off with his big tongue. But the chocolate letters were still there, and Sebastian's mommy said, "Sebastian has become a prophet for our family. He speaks in the name of Life and continually invites us to embrace Life and dance with it. The dance of Life has very complex steps, and sometimes we fall flat on our faces, but our little prophet is there to remind us that Life can take a tumble and recover. On this Mother's Day, we wish to give Sebastian an extra name, to acknowledge what he does for us. The Bible tells us that Isaiah was a great prophet who spoke in the name of the Lord, which is another name for Life. So please welcome Isaiah, our official prophet. We are all truly blessed to have him."

By that time, all the big people were crying and looking at the cake. Some of the letters were gone, Sebastian having finished working on the sun, but my mommy could still read what was written: "Thank you, Isaiah." She explained to me what that meant. I understood very well, but I could also see that somebody had to start cutting the cake before the prophet ate all the icing. So I very politely said that I was very hungry for cake. Madeleine – that's Sebastian's mommy – said that eating the cake now was a very good idea: the celebration of Life can take many forms. Anna was asked to cut the cake because she knew a lot sooner than her mommy and daddy that Sebastian is a prophet. I got the letters "u" and "I," which are very good letters.

I was looking forward to telling Grandma about our Mother's Day party at Sebastian's home, especially since I had not really understood all that was going on. It's hard to understand things when you are in the presence of a chocolate cake that might disappear into the mouth of a prophet, and nobody realizes that you are very hungry. So I missed some of it. Grandma was very interested in what I had to say – she always is. I suspect that she thinks of me as a little prophet in my own family, but she knows that I don't have the official qualifications, so she doesn't say it out loud. She explained to me that people have dreams. Some dreams visit you during the night. Some are really good, especially those that involve flying around in an airplane. Some are not so good, like when some bad people sneak up on you and you don't have your mommy and daddy with you. That happens most often if your teddy bear has also fallen asleep and can't watch over you. During the day, dreams don't visit people. It's people who visit their dreams, and unlike the night dreams, people have the choice of what and who will be in their dreams. Daydreams are very good things. People should be encouraged to make a lot of them during the day. However, some problems may develop.

Life also has dreams for people. That as such is not necessarily a problem, but sometimes the dreams that Life has for people don't go well with the dreams that the people have made up for themselves. What happens then is that the dreams start to fight to see which one will be the strongest. The people whose dreams are fighting with the dreams Life has for them really feel the fight inside of them. They feel that their dreams have been pushed aside to make room for Life's dreams, and this can hurt very badly and for a very long time. Sometimes the people get very angry at Life because they feel Life has made a mistake and made up a very bad dream for them. People try to get Life to back off with the dreams that are not suitable for them, but Life is very strong and has much experience. Life insists that people take the dreams that It has made up for them. That can be hard to do, especially since Life likes to move around in mysterious ways – you can't always know where It is coming from, so It seems to have all the advantages.

However, in the great battle of dreams, Life will provide people with what they need to have the dreams make peace. Life provides people with the capacity to contemplate and create meaning. You might think that is not much of a tool when there is a battle of dreams raging inside of you, but it is. And if people learn to use that tool, they may one day discover that the dreams that Life has chosen for them can live together with the dreams they had made for themselves. That may take some time, especially since Life likes a lot of mystery and is often hard to figure out, but it can be done. As a matter of fact, people do it all the time. Sebastian's mommy and daddy did not dream of having a little boy with a big tongue and a hole in his heart and funny eyes. But Life thought they could use a prophet, so It sent Sebastian along. Of course, at first, Sebastian's mommy and daddy were not able to see the prophet that was waiting to be seen. They could only see their pain and the loss of their dream. But gradually, they were able to see better and even see what nobody else could see. One day, they realized that they had been living with a loving prophet who spoke in the name of Life. They had to celebrate, of course, and that's how we came to be blessed with a very good chocolate cake. Grandma always says that chocolate is one of the best side-effects of Life.

"out of my dreams and into my life you came"

Out of my dreams and into my life you came.

I opened my arms to welcome you

Only to realize that you had come from a very

bad dream.

I closed my eyes so I could not see you

And went back to sleep

To give you another chance to come out of my dreams

And into my life.

When I awoke again, you were still there,

Exactly as before.

Again I closed my eyes so I could not see you

And I wished to fall asleep

To give you another chance to come out of my dreams

And into my life.

When I awoke again, you were still there,

Exactly as before.

I was just closing my eyes again when

        I heard you calling,

"Mommy, Mommy, I know you are in there.

Come out of your dreams and into my life."

I finally opened my eyes and saw you

As beautiful as you are, and so much more beautiful

Than you were in the best of dreams.

And I finally came into your life.

16

Creating meanings:

An adventure

I had quite an adventure last week. In case you don't know exactly what an adventure is, it's like a story in a storybook, except you can't peek at the last few pages to see what happens to the little boy who got lost in the forest. Some adventures are really nice and some can be quite scary. The one last week was very nice but also very scary. One thing you can be sure of with every kind of adventure is that there will be many surprises.

The adventure started after breakfast. My mommy and daddy told me to find my hat and put on my running shoes because we were going out to celebrate a very big birthday. I need help to put on my shoes because my left foot doesn't always know which is its shoe, though my right foot usually knows which is its shoe. While my daddy was helping me, he explained that today was our country's birthday, and we would go to a big party on a hill. A country is like a big, big family, except that the big family doesn't fit into one house, so the people from the family live in many, many houses, and it is very hard to visit them all. Sometimes the people in the big, big family miss the other people that they don't have time to visit. Sometimes they don't miss them.

I went up to my room to get my crocodile. I like adventures, generally, but since I don't know what will actually happen, I find it safe to bring my crocodile with me, just in case. My crocodile looks like he's made of rubber because he is very soft and can take many shapes, but *I* know that he is entirely made of crocodile. Grandma once explained that my crocodile has given me help many times, and that all the help that he has given me is now inside of me. I can use that help anytime I need it, even though my crocodile is not with me. That may be, but I like to have my crocodile by my side so people can see his many teeth.

My mommy and daddy packed a lunch, and we set off on our adventure. The first surprise was that we didn't get in the car. We walked down the street and waited for a little while on the corner, and then we got on a big red-and-white bus. I had never had the honour of taking a bus before, but I had seen them quite often and was happy to take one. I thought there might be a TV on the bus because everybody was looking in the same direction. Well, there is no TV on the bus. It's not necessary at all because there are many windows and you can look out and see many things, including the tops of the cars. We got on the bus, and my parents invited me to choose a seat. I chose a really nice one and held on tight to my daddy's hand. After a little while, I chose another seat and we all moved there. And then we tried even more seats during our trip. It was so exciting. There were many other people on the bus who were all on an adventure of their own.

When we got to the party place, my mommy suggested I say thank you to the bus driver for the nice ride. The bus driver said that I was welcome, and she hoped I would get to take her bus another time. We got off and my daddy told me to look around to choose what I wanted to see. He also said that I must always hold his hand tightly so I wouldn't get lost. So I led the way. First we visited a clown who was half scary and half funny and who offered to paint a flag on my face. I wasn't too sure at first if I wanted him to because of the half-scary part, but I said he could. The clown showed me his work with a mirror. I must say I was quite pleased with the results. After that, we went to see a place where the people were making all kinds of animals with balloons. Then my mommy gave me a big ice cream cone with chocolate on top. That was another surprise because we hadn't even had our lunch yet. Then we found a place to sit on our blanket and listen to people who were singing songs. Some people were dancing and waving their arms.

I wasn't dancing because I needed to rest after my long journey, so I was just sitting there, enjoying the music, when a big girl who was dancing stepped on my hand and it hurt. I turned towards my crocodile to have him scare away the big girl, but he wasn't there. My tummy immediately became very trembly and my eyes started hurting and I couldn't see very well. I started crying. Right away, my mommy and daddy helped me look for my crocodile, but he wasn't under the blanket or in the picnic basket or in my daddy's jacket pocket. He was nowhere. If you've ever lost your crocodile, you will know what it does to your body. Losing your crocodile is like your body being turned upside down, but much worse.

My daddy took me in his arms and said we should go back to the places we had visited to see if the crocodile had stayed behind. I could tell that my parents were very worried about my crocodile. My mommy picked up the blanket and picnic basket and we started walking all around. Every place we went, we couldn't find my crocodile, and every time we didn't find it, I became even more afraid, which is strange, since right at the beginning of not finding my crocodile, I was already as afraid as I could possibly be. A couple of times, I thought about Prince Igor and how he must have felt when the bad people took his teddy bear away, and it made me cry even more. When we had gone to all the places, I stopped crying because I was very tired, and my daddy said to me, "Felix, even though you can't see your crocodile, why don't you ask him where he is and if he would like to be found?" You might think that is a strange thing to say, but my daddy works with people who are able to hear voices coming from people nobody can see, and he has learned a lot from them.

So I called out, "Crocodile, where are you?" But my crocodile didn't answer me. I called out again and again, and all of a sudden, my crocodile told my mommy where he might be found. I think my crocodile gave the answer to my mommy because she wasn't as busy as I was. All she had to do was hold the blanket and the picnic basket. My mommy said, "Felix, we haven't seen your crocodile since we were on the bus. Maybe he stayed on the bus." And then, I sort of saw a picture of the last seat we had tried, and my crocodile was there, looking out the window at all the people who were having an adventure that day. I told this to my daddy and mommy, and my daddy made us wait for him while he walked over to the bus stop. We couldn't see him, but it seems he spoke to the driver of one of the buses. The driver understood what was going on because he had small children, and he called the lady who knows where all the city buses are. The lady said that my crocodile had been found and had travelled on the bus to the bus garage. My daddy said that the crocodile was okay, though he was very tired after the long trip. The people at the garage were taking good care of him. I just hoped that they wouldn't try to feed him broccoli.

We stayed a bit longer at the party, but I was not enjoying myself as much even though there were airplanes making some kind of dance in the sky. So my mommy and daddy and I decided to go home. We took the bus again. I didn't get to see much of the sights because I fell asleep. Worrying about somebody who is important to you is very tiring. My mommy had to wake me up to get off the bus and walk home. Then my daddy and I took the car and we went to the bus garage to get my crocodile. My crocodile had been put on a special shelf reserved for important animals, and he was sleeping. I made him say thank you to the nice people, and I never let go of his hand till we got home. I even brought him to bed with me that night just to make sure he wouldn't escape again.

Grandma listened carefully to the story of my adventure. She likes my crocodile a lot because of all the help he brings me. She also likes adventures and has had several of her own, though never in a desert like Prince Igor. She explained to me that Life is a great big adventure, so big that you can't see all of it at the same time. You might know how the adventure of your Life started, but you don't know how it will end – it is just too big. But since it's fun to know how an adventure ends, you can have a great number of *little* adventures and see how they end. All your little adventures add up to become part of the great adventure of Life. (You remember that Life is what makes people move during their adventures.)

The most interesting part of an adventure is actually the end, says Grandma, because the end of an adventure is a mystery, and mysteries keep you from being bored. I knew that already because Grandma really loves mysteries, especially since she stopped feeling she should try to understand them. Some mysteries really annoy her, she tells me, but she has decided to take the annoying mysteries with the nice ones.

So I get to hear quite a bit about mysteries. But then Grandma told me something surprising. She said that you can actually change the ending of an adventure once the adventure is over. For instance, the ending of my adventure at the country party could be that I have learned a very important thing, which is never to let go of my crocodile's hand while travelling with him. The ending of my adventure could also be that during this hard time I got all the help I needed from my mommy and my daddy, and that it feels so good to know that they are there. Or the ending of my adventure could be that the world is full of people who are willing to help each other, and that I can grow up to be one of these people.

So there are many possible endings to an adventure, and you can choose one or the other or several at a time if you want to. You can even choose an ending and keep that ending for a while, and then decide that you want to change it for some reason. It's up to you. A person could even choose an ending that does not feel good or help this person at all. For instance, I could choose to think I have been a bad little boy because I did not take care of my crocodile. But why would I choose this ending when there are other endings that will help me learn and grow well? While Grandma was on the subject of adventures, I suggested that we check on what was happening to Prince Igor. The last time we saw him, he was travelling on a mountain and had been invited to a big feast. The interesting thing about this feast is that the people who had invited him suggested that he bring his camel to the table with him to enjoy the feast in complete peace.

"My dearest grandson"

My dearest grandson,
As you are taking off to see the world
And, hopefully, save it,
I must give you some wise parting words.
The very words that my grandmother gave me
When, as a young man like you,
I took off to see the world.

"Goodbye, my dearest," said my grandmother.
"Be safe, and take very good care of your underwear."
"Take very good care of my underwear?!
What do you mean?"

But my grandmother never was one who felt the need
To explain her actions or her thoughts.
So she just hugged me goodbye.

I travelled the world.
I climbed snow-capped mountains,
Dived in the deepest seas,
Crossed deserts and plains,
Fought my way through villages and cities,
Ate all kinds of strange delicacies,
Caught all sorts of fevers,
Knew pain and loss, discovery and elation.
And all through my adventures,
In loving memory of my grandmother who passed away
While I was in darkest Africa,
I took very good care of my underwear.

On the way home I met your grandmother,
And the real adventure started then:
The adventure of raising your father and his sisters.
We always lived in the same city, in the same house,
But your father and his sisters sure made
        their parents travel!
Today, I am seeing you off on your adventure
And I say to you:
"Goodbye, my dearest. Be safe.
And take good care of what nobody can see
That is yours and nobody else's.
Take care of what is close to you
And touches you gently.
Take good care of your underwear."

17

Playing just for fun:

Invisible toys

Last Sunday was Happy Father's Day. That day has been invented to help the daddies remember how happy they are to have little children. Daddies can become very tired and forget how happy they are to have little children. So it's good for them, once in a while, to be reminded of their happiness. I must say, though, that my daddy has never forgotten how happy he is to have me. I know this because he often plays with me without my having to ask him.

So last Sunday morning my daddy woke me up early. We had breakfast because even on a special day, everyone in our house has to eat a good breakfast. We sat together and made plans for the day, while my mommy was still sleeping. Mommy likes to sleep in on Happy Father's Day. Daddy suggested we go out and play for the day, or at least the morning. We didn't have to decide right away. When you are playing, you don't have to decide everything in advance; it would be too much like work. I asked Daddy if we were going out on our tricycles, but he said no, we would be going on foot. I also asked which toys to bring, but he said we would bring nothing, just ourselves. That would be enough, he said, because when we bring just ourselves, our bodies and ideas come along automatically, and that's all we need for play.

When it was time to leave for our play day, we went to the front door. Just as we were going to open it, Daddy said: "You know, Felix, people who play well and often like to do things upside down. Good ideas for play often start with doing things upside down. If you do everything right side up, you might get into the habit of working all the time. Not a good habit at all." So Daddy suggested that we go out by another door, or even a window, just to get used to doing things upside down. I chose the window in the room where I keep my toys because I know this window very well. I look through it all the time. It seemed strange to go through a window when we could go through the door, but I sort of liked the idea because my daddy was with me. I hoped that the neighbours would see us. It would make them happy to see us playing.

We started walking down the street, and then Daddy stopped in front of Jaime's house. Jaime has two mommies and they all live in the same house because his two mommies like each other. You might think that having two mommies would mean having two daddies, as my friend Martin does, but no. There are no daddies in that house. So Daddy said, "Let's invite Jaime to join us on our play day, because he has no happy daddy today." I like Jaime, though I find that one of his mommies doesn't laugh enough. So I said, "Sure." We rang the doorbell and found that Jaime was already prepared to come out with us. My daddy told him not to bring anything but himself; that's how it was today. Jaime understood right away even though he's not used to having a daddy tell him what to do. He said, "Sure," waved goodbye to his two mommies, and off we went.

We continued to walk down the street. After a while, we came to the park, just as I was wondering if we had started playing yet. Sometimes, with my daddy, it's hard to know when we are playing and when we aren't. I thought we would play on the swings in the park, but Daddy just continued through the park. We crossed the park and came to the block where Martin has one of his houses. Martin is my friend who has two daddies, two houses, two brothers, but only one dog. Because of this, Martin knows many more things than I do, and it's a bit scary at times. Daddy said to Jaime and me, "Martin has two daddies, but today the daddy in this house has to sleep because he had to work at a big fire last night, so he doesn't have time to be happy today. His other daddy is in the other house and can't come out to play. I'm sure Martin wouldn't mind spending the day with us – he's used to having more than one daddy, so it won't be a problem for him." Well, would you believe it? Martin was right at the door, all ready to join our play day.

I let Martin walk on the other side of my daddy, and Jaime held my other hand. And off we went again. I still didn't know if we were playing yet, but I had a feeling that we might be because I felt like there was a smile inside my tummy. We walked further down the street, towards Michaela's house. Michaela has a daddy at her house, but he can't walk because his legs don't work well, and he can't play games where you need your legs. He still remembers that he is happy to have little children, but sometimes he forgets, and then he cries and Michaela doesn't like that. Today he was not crying at all, and he told Michaela to have a good time on the play day. He gave her a big hug so she knew he meant it.

We walked back to the park, and my daddy asked all of us to choose a tree that could tell us something. We didn't know what he meant at first, so he explained that if we listen carefully, some trees can talk to us. Martin chose the biggest tree, and we all agreed that that was a very good idea. We sat down with our backs to the tree and Daddy told us to be very quiet and feel how the tree was glad to see us on Happy Father's Day. We could feel it with our backs or our arms and hands if we stretched them out against the tree. Michaela said the tree was making a noise like a tiny little motor, and Jaime said that it felt like there were bumblebees in the tree. We all started to scream when we heard about the bumblebees, but Daddy made us be quiet again. He explained that the tree had made Jaime *think* of bumblebees, but that didn't mean that there were some there.

Then my daddy had us lie down at the foot of the big tree and we looked at the sky through the branches. He had us look for triangles first and then for pictures of animals in the leaves and branches. I was the first one to spot the duck, though Martin said it was a chicken. I gave Martin a shove to show him what a duck is, and Martin gave me a kick on the leg. My daddy immediately sat between us and had us both find our animals again. Daddy explained that a spot in the tree can be both a duck and a chicken – it depends on how you look. He said that that spot reminded him of a teapot. I didn't think that was fair because we were not looking for kitchen stuff.

After that, we looked at the clouds to see pretty pictures. I saw a very nice teddy bear, but the more I looked at it, the more it became like a crocodile. And then we played shadow tag. In shadow tag you run after shadows, and it's fun because you can step on somebody's shadow without hurting it. If you are tired of running, you can go under the big tree. The big tree's shadow will hide your shadow for you, so you can't get caught.

By that time, we had played a lot, and playing takes lots of energy, so we were getting hungry. Daddy decided we should go to our house and see if there was anything to eat. When we got home, Jaime's mommies were there, and Michaela's, too. Martin's daddy was also there because he had finished his nap and wanted to be a Happy Father with Martin. I was glad of this because Martin is always nicer when he has one of his daddies nearby. My mommy and all the other big people had prepared a nice lunch that did not involve too many vegetables. And then we had a Happy Father's Day cake with lots of letters on the icing. After a while, everybody went back to their homes, and I agreed with my mommy that I needed a nap. My mommy and I usually don't agree about naps, but this time I was willing to take one. For one thing, I was tired because play is hard work. Also, I wanted to see nice pictures in my head, and for this you need peace and quiet.

Grandma was very pleased to know that my daddy and I had gone out to play on Happy Father's Day. She knows that parents work very hard to take good care of their little children, and even their bigger ones, so she likes to hear that the daddies are happy in spite of all that work. She wanted to know exactly when and how I knew I was playing. Nobody could tell at first glance that I was playing, since I was not using my toys or my ball or my tricycle. And yet I had played a lot on that outing. When had the playing started, she asked? I didn't know how to answer, so Grandma asked me another question to help me. "What is the first thing you did that was really different from what you usually do?" I knew the answer to that one: it was when we climbed out the window to leave the house. It felt really strange: a tiny bit scary and funny. I wanted our neighbours to see us, and yet I was a bit shy about it. Grandma thought that was probably the moment when I had started to play, and that I knew about it when I felt there was a little smile in my tummy. Often, when you start playing, it feels a bit strange. That is because the rules for playing are not the same as the rules for working. When you are playing, you pretty much make up the rules as you go along, and though that can be very exciting, it does feel funny, especially if you are new at this or you haven't played in a long while.

Grandma explained that playing with invisible toys is very convenient. When your toys are inside you, they don't weigh anything and they don't take up space in your backpack that could be used for snacks and extra clothes if you are at an age when you might need a sudden change of clothes. The toys inside you allow you to see everyday things and people in a new and interesting way so you never ever get bored. With a good set of toys inside of you, you can make up new pictures whenever you need them, and that is very helpful when you are trying to finish a puzzle. I understood that because when I was more little, one of my puzzles was missing a big piece. One day my mommy found the piece in the hole in the floor where the air from the furnace comes out, and I finally got to see the other part of the lion. (I must say that I am not crazy about furnaces because they live in the dark.)

Grandma said that some people think that play and work can't get along together, but they can. Just imagine a tiny Christmas tree with lots of red lights on one side (that would be the work side), and lots of blue lights on the other side (that would be the play side). If you turn the tree slowly, you will see red lights, then blue lights, then red lights again, and that is pretty enough. But if you turn the tree very fast, it will look like the tree is covered in pretty purple lights, and that is super pretty, especially since purple is my favourite colour. The toys inside you are what allow work and play to lighten up together.

"I watch you play"

I watch you play

So studiously and yet so freely.

You don't seem to understand that train engines

Are what run on tracks, not airplanes.

You don't seem to understand that puzzles

Are meant to be assembled with the picture side up.

You don't seem to understand

That blocks from a set should go on belonging to that set.

You don't seem to understand

That teddy bears don't eat trucks, no matter how small.

You don't seem to understand

That a piano bench is not an open-sided tunnel.

You don't seem to understand

That a banana is a fruit, not a telephone receiver.

You just don't understand the rules of play.

And suddenly I wonder what happened to me.

Where did I learn

That instructions have to be followed or else?

Where did I learn that deadlines must always be met

And rules never, ever be broken?

Where did I learn that everything in life

Should be put back into its box?

Where did I learn that things must always go

In one direction – the right one, of course?

When did I stop thinking, feeling, daring, inventing?

You look up at me

With that beautiful smile that goes right up

      to your eyes.

"Daddy, come play with me."

"Oh, yes, yes, PLEASE."

18

Saying goodbye:

The death of a pet

The whole street knows about what happened to Felicia and her family two weeks ago, but in case you don't live on our street, I will tell you all about it. You will be interested because this story is about a little dog and also because it is a sad story. Sad stories can be quite interesting because they can make you feel really glad you have a mommy and a daddy. In that way, sad stories can become glad stories, though you don't know this at the beginning of the story.

The story happened two weeks ago, but it started before that. Felicia received a little puppy as a gift from her mommy and daddy. It was their way of saying they were sorry for having gotten a little brother for her when she had specifically asked for a little sister. Felicia does not have a very high opinion of boys, having a big brother and also two cousins who are boys. I must say, though, that Felicia likes me even though she knows I am a boy. That is probably because I like Felicia even though she is a girl.

Felicia named her puppy Petunia. Had she consulted me on the choice of her puppy's name, I would have suggested a real dog name, like Croco or Speedo, but Felicia is an independent thinker, and she didn't ask for my opinion. I gave it anyway, and we sort of had a little fight, but it didn't last long. I find that I don't like to fight with my friends who have a puppy or a dog. They wouldn't let me play with them if I fight. Once we agreed that Petunia was the right name for the puppy, Felicia let me hold it and play with it when we visited her.

Then the terrible thing happened. One afternoon, Felicia's mommy was backing up the car in the driveway, and she was going very slowly because that's how mommies and daddies back up their cars. She checked carefully that Felicia's big brother had not left his bicycle in the driveway, as he has been known to do. But she couldn't see that Petunia had found a way to escape under the backyard fence and was standing in the driveway. Felicia's mommy hit Petunia with the car. All of Petunia's legs were broken except two. Felicia's mommy cried out for help, and Felicia's daddy and a neighbour came right away. The neighbour offered to take care of the baby. Felicia, her mommy and her daddy put Petunia in a blanket and took her to the dog hospital. Felicia thought that the doctor would fix Petunia's legs like he had fixed her big brother's arm when he had fallen out of the tree. But then the terrible thing became even more terrible because the doctor said that Petunia's back was also broken and that he would have to put Petunia to sleep. Felicia's daddy explained that was another way of saying that the dog was too hurt to live anymore and that she was going to die. Felicia thought she knew about dying because she had watched the movie where the baby lion's daddy dies, and she had seen some real-live dead animals on the road they took to visit her grandparents. But she discovered she knew absolutely nothing about Petunia dying. It was awful.

Meanwhile, everybody on the street who likes dogs or Felicia's family got to know about this terrible situation. My mommy told me about it, and I felt as terrible as the situation. We kept an eye on the street, and when we saw that Felicia's car was back, we walked over to talk to Felicia and her family to say we were sorry and to ask if we could help. My daddy explained that this is what we do when somebody we know has received a terrible situation. Felicia's daddy said that Felicia was okay. She was having a snack right now, and would I join her? Felicia's mommy ran into my mommy's arms. She was crying and saying over and over again, "I feel so guilty." My mommy was saying over and over again, "It's not your fault, you couldn't know, it was an accident," but that didn't stop the crying. I didn't know what "guilty" meant, but I decided not to ask. It could wait till the next time I saw Grandma.

Felicia and I had a nice snack, and she told me all about the dog doctor and how it went. From what I understand, dead people are disappeared people, and I wanted to know if Petunia had already disappeared. I also wanted to know if the doctor had put Petunia in the recycle bin. Felicia said that was the stupidest idea she had ever heard in her whole life. She said that the doctor would put Petunia in a nice restful place till she disappeared completely. Her whole family would go to her grandmother's to get a tree from her forest and plant the tree in the backyard in memory of Petunia. That was what her daddy had said. Well, if that isn't recycling, I don't know what is. I told Felicia that my recycling bin idea was not so stupid after all. Felicia said that I was through with my snack at this very instant.

After a while we went home because it was getting close to my bedtime and also because life goes on, as my daddy said on the way home. I very much like the idea of life going on, but that night I wished life didn't have to start going on with a bedtime. Bedtime is not the best of times on most days, and that night it was especially not a best time. My head and heart were too full with that terrible situation, and there was not enough space in my bed for all of that. My animals had to sleep on the floor, except, of course, for my teddy bear. My mommy and daddy both put me to bed together. Usually, if they are both involved in putting me to bed, they take turns because it's one of those nights, as they like to say. That night, they wanted to make sure I was okay. That's how bad stories start changing into glad stories.

The following day, I asked Felicia if her parents were going to get her another dog. She said that right away after the accident her mother had said they would. But later, after they knew that Petunia would become a disappeared dog, Felicia's daddy said it would be up to Felicia to decide. She should decide only when Petunia had disappeared enough to leave enough room for another dog. He said Felicia would know inside her heart when it was the right time. At that time, Petunia would have completely disappeared, but she would have started to appear in Felicia's heart, a bit like a friendly spirit. Felicia is very interested in spirits. She even dressed up as a ghost last Halloween. It's usually boys who do that.

A few days later, Felicia said that many people had said nice things to her about Petunia, but some people had said things that she didn't understand or that were just plain stupid. When Felicia says something or somebody is stupid, she means it. Some people said that the puppy had gone to doggy heaven. That didn't help Felicia at all because she has no idea where doggy heaven is. To her, it was completely useless information. I understand that. When my mommy goes out, she always tells me where she is going and when she will be back. The only part that really interests me is the "when she will be coming back" part. Where she is going doesn't interest me. If I am in a mood to miss her, I'll miss her, wherever she is going. So Felicia was given the useless information about where the puppy had gone, but not the important information about when the puppy would come back. That was before she had completely understood that disappearing means not coming back, ever.

Grandma liked this story because she likes sad stories that become glad stories. I suspect she has quite a bit of experience with those kinds of stories because she is very old. She was also a little sad, too, because she likes little dogs, though not as much as she likes little children. And she is always a little sad when she hears I've been through a terrible situation. She explained what "guilty" means. It's how I feel when I know I have done something that might get me a major time out. When I become very quiet so my daddy and mommy won't hear me, and I hide behind something or go into another room so they can't see me, it is a pretty good sign that I'm doing something I'll end up feeling guilty about. Grandma explained that guilt can help me learn to behave better. At least that's what she hopes.

When something terrible happens, people often react by blaming themselves, even if the terrible thing is not their fault. It doesn't seem to be a very useful thing to do, especially in the case of an accident, like the one that happened to Petunia. You have to wonder why they do that. Grandma explained that most mommies and daddies love their children so much that it's very hard when something terrible happens to them. Parents want with all their hearts to take away the pain. If they think the pain came because they've done something wrong, they think all they have to do is behave better and that will prevent all accidents and terrible situations. Of course that doesn't happen. That is called an illusion. An illusion is like a dream you have when you are not sleeping.

After this discussion, we needed to check on Prince Igor to see if he was doing all right. When something bad happens to someone you like, like Felicia and Petunia, you want to make sure that the other people that you like are fine. Well, Prince Igor was okay, though he still worries about his teddy bear (and who wouldn't?), but he has been given another hint by a Spirit about where the bad people have put his bear. Grandma hasn't yet said what the hint is. It's a little mystery.

"Till death do us part"

"Till death do us part."
We read that contract and added in fine print,
"But only when we are very old
And have had many children and grandchildren."

But apparently cancer is illiterate.
Or perhaps it won't read the fine print
Or it just doesn't care about contracts,
children and grandchildren.

"Have faith," you said as you were going away.
"I will never leave you.
I will be behind every tree
And around every corner."

I look for you always, everywhere
And yet I can't see you.
I cry out to you
And I don't hear you answer.
I turn to touch you
And my hand touches an empty space.

But our child, your beloved child,

The one with your smile and your eyes

Sees you, hears you, touches you

All the time, all over the place.

"Look, Mommy, a deer on the side of the road.

It must be Daddy."

"Listen, Mommy, the night bird is singing a new song.

It must be Daddy."

"Touch this beautiful stone, Mommy.

Daddy must have sent it to us."

Dear Lord,

Give me the eyes, the ears and the hands of a child.

NOW. PLEASE.

19

Riding the rails:

A train trip

You might find this hard to believe, but yesterday I took a train trip! You might think I am inventing this since I am quite young and have been known to occasionally have trouble distinguishing dreams from reality, but this is a very true story. I don't know if you have had the opportunity to take a train before. If you haven't, I strongly recommend that you make arrangements right away to do so. You will not regret it, I assure you. If possible, bring a young child with you. Perhaps you do not know that very young people are allowed to travel on trains. I didn't know this before my trip, but on the train I actually saw two babies, one with a daddy and the other one with a mommy. This is just to say that it is never too early to get into the habit of taking the train with small children.

What happened is that a few days ago, my mommy, my daddy, my dog Pilfroy (the one that nobody can see but me) and I went to the train station to greet my grandmother, who had travelled from far away to come visit us. I call this grandmother "Granny," as this is her name and she is a different grandmother from the one I call "Grandma." At this point in my life, I have met two of my grandmothers. Grandma always says that it's very nice to have several grandmothers; in fact, according to her, a person cannot have too many grandmothers. Grandma says that when I grow up, I will meet many other grandmothers if I need to, and they can all be very nice and helpful. So Grandma was really happy that Granny was coming to visit us. Granny has visited us already a few times, and when she leaves our house, I miss her quite a bit. I don't always remember her between visits, but when I see her again, I remember that I had remembered her.

We got to the train station, parked the car and went in. I made Pilfroy stay in the car because all dogs in a train station have to be in a suitcase with holes in it. I know he would have hated that. We went to a window to watch the big train arrive on the tracks. The train opened its doors and out came Granny with many other people. The other people didn't belong to us, though. We ran to her and she gave us big hugs and said how much I have grown and time flies so fast. We piled Granny and the suitcases into the car and we came home. Everyone was excited, even Pilfroy, though he had to sit on my lap because Granny had taken his place.

I talked about the train the whole evening. I do know a lot about trains, having many engines and wagons, but I had never actually been on a big train. So Granny then had a great idea: one day, pretty soon, she would take me on a train, so I would know what it was like. Well, the pretty-soon day turned out to be yesterday, so that's how I can tell you all about it. Mommy and Pilfroy drove us to the station, but they didn't park the car. They just left us there. Granny talked to a nice lady who gave us tickets for the train, and then we heard a loud voice say that it was time to get on the train. I was very excited but not scared at all, though I had left my protector crocodile at home. A granny can provide even better help than a crocodile if there is a danger, especially that granny.

Once we were on the train, we chose our seats. I had my best shoes on, so there was no danger of putting mud on the seats. I mention this because a young child can't travel by train without some standing on the seats. The man from the train came to see me to say hello, and he gave me a colouring book containing lots of useful information about train engines. I said thank you, but I decided to put the book in my backpack because I was more interested in looking out the window. Trains may have been invented to get people to take time to look through windows.

Granny has travelled a lot by train, so she knew exactly what the best features are. The very best feature, according to her, is that by look-ing out the window, you get to see new things all the time. All the very interesting things are lined up and ready to appear in your window. But you won't see all of them unless *you* move. That's why a train is so useful: you get to move without even moving from your own seat. It is much less tiring than if you had to walk or take your tricycle to see the lineup of the interesting things. When you're tired, you have to take a nap or a long night's sleep, and while you are sleeping, some interesting things might be happening, and you will miss them. Sleep is a subject of some disagreement between my mommy and me. She believes that tomorrow will be a new day. I can see her point, of course, but I hate to start a new day when I haven't yet finished with the old one.

There is one problem with travelling in a train. Sometimes it goes so fast that you don't have the time to see all the interesting things. So Granny helped me a lot at first by pointing out the more special things. She pointed out a building made like a tower where they put the food for the cows. It's like a big, big round refrigerator, but there is no milk in the refrigerator, just cereal. The farmers keep the milk in the cows. Then Granny had me play "I spy with my little eye." "I spy" is harder than just looking at something that has been pointed out to you because it's your little eye that has to do the pointing. But I like that game anyway. It's more grown-up.

After a while, the train man came to offer us some food and drinks. I took an apple juice and a ham sandwich because it's easy with a ham sandwich to tell exactly what's in it. Granny also took a sandwich – I didn't bother to ask what kind – and a coffee. I have noticed on several occasions that when big people have a coffee, it's because they have stopped what they were doing and have not yet started to do what they will be doing next. A coffee is the difference between before and after. So, naturally, I was curious to see what Granny was going to do next. Not seeing Granny that often, I don't know her well enough to guess what was coming.

After finishing her coffee, Granny sighed a big sigh because she was so full of happiness she was in danger of exploding if she didn't let some of it out. I sighed, too, because I, too, was full of happiness and ham sandwich. Then Granny said to me, "Felix, children are so much better at seeing interesting things than many big people are. When some people become older, their eyes get so used to seeing certain things, that after a while they can see only those things. Their lineup of interesting things becomes a lot shorter, and they can't see all the other things that are not in that lineup. It's as if they were travelling in their own train, but that train had stopped moving. Maybe this doesn't happen to all big people, but I know it does to me once in a while. When I realize this is happening, I must find a way to get my eyes to see better and farther. Today, you can help my eyes see better by pointing out interesting things that I have not noticed. So it's your turn. Go!"

Well, the first thing I thought Granny would be interested in is what is under a train seat. If you look under things, very often your head has to be upside down and that already makes these things look funny. Plus, things under things are bound to be interesting because they are often in some kind of dark. Dark, as you know, can be scary, but if dark is next to something really interesting, you won't get a trembly tummy, just a surprised tummy. The seats on the train were very interesting especially after Granny asked the nice train man to turn our seats so we could look in the other direction. With the seats turned in another direction, all that was in the lineup came as a surprise from the back.

Then I took Granny to explore the rest of the train. I didn't know the rest of the train, but I made things up as needed so Granny would enjoy the exploration. I discovered I could be quite a good guide, even though for many things it was the first time I had seen them. For example, the bathrooms were very weird and noisy, but Granny wasn't afraid of them because I was there. The most interesting thing that I showed Granny is the space between the wagons where the doors are. Granny wondered if in that space we were still on the train. I took her hand because I could feel she was a little afraid of the answer to that question.

After that, we went back to our seats to catch up on the lineup. I thought we must have missed many things during our exploration of the train, but Granny explained that there were lineups all the time, all over the place, as long as we kept our eyes open. I pointed out several things to Granny from the lineup: many brown cows and their babies, a big lake near a barn, and a dog running across a field. The dog reminded me of Pilfroy, my dog that nobody else can see, so I brought Pilfroy on the train with me for a few minutes. Then I had him go home because dogs are not allowed on trains where there are little children. The children can upset the dogs. After a while, we came to a city with many houses. I had Granny look at the spaces between the houses. She liked that because she likes to see the sky even if it is for a very short moment during a train ride.

Granny thanked me for helping her see things that she had forgotten to look at, and she told me to put my shoes back on because at the next station we would be getting off the train. I must say that up till then I hadn't realized that we would get off the train and that it would continue without us. I wondered if the lineups would go on with the train or if they would follow me. The train stopped, we said goodbye to the nice train man, and we got off the train. I didn't know what we would do next because we were not back in our own city. Then I saw that my mommy and my Grandma, the one who is not Granny, were waiting for us. They had come in the car to get us. But before we started heading back home, Grandma said that we had to celebrate that Granny and I had had such a lovely adventure. She took us all to the ice cream store so we could make the celebrations official. I chose a chocolate ice cream cone. I prefer to eat ice cream in a cone rather than a bowl because if the ice cream drips from the cone onto your arms or T-shirt, you are allowed to lick it off. At our house, licking food off things is considered bad manners.

When we got home, I found Pilfroy waiting for me. He was glad he had been able to come on the train, even for a short while. I discussed the whole trip with him rather than with Grandma because Grandma already knew everything about the trip. Granny had told her all about it.

"My life with you is like a train trip"

My life with you is like a train trip.

We sit together, gently talk and enjoy the view.

And all of a sudden, you jump up.

"Hey, where are you going?"

"I must get off here. I have something to do.

I'll be back in a while."

And, in your own time, you do come back.

You must be our own stationmaster,

Because the train starts moving again

As soon as you climb back in.

The train pulls out of the station

And I glance at its name: "Learning to share."

We become once again good travelling companions.
Our train travels gently through the countryside.
All is well. And then suddenly, again:
"I must get off here. I have something to do.
I'll be back in a while."
And off you go once more, by yourself.
And then you reappear.
The train pulls out of the station,
And I glance at its name: "Learning to Accept."

I pull out the itinerary:
Learning to love, to respect, to give,
To create, to experiment, to communicate,
To play, to receive, to refuse, to work…
— And this is only the first page of the itinerary.

There are so many other stations where you will get off
To learn what you must learn.
I am the one who will be stationary
And wait as patiently as I can
Till you give the signal to move together again.

At this rate of travel, our trip together will last
a very long time.
And be assured that I am not about to complain!

20

Being sick yet so alive:

Illness

The other Sunday, I went to the Teddy Bears' picnic. You might think that I am saying that I brought my teddy bear to a picnic. That is not it at all. It is I who accompanied my teddy bear to a picnic organized especially for teddy bears who are sick or hurt. My teddy bear is not sick, though he will tire easily if he has had to work hard during the night to keep an eye on me when the bad dreams want to come up through the windows. But he was having a problem with a detaching ear, and my parents thought he might benefit from attending a picnic intended especially for teddy bears who have been working too hard. The fresh air and the games would take his mind off things.

You must understand that a picnic, as such, is not enough to fix a detaching ear. A picnic can help with bad dreams, trembly tummies, missing Granny and Grandpa and things like that, but it won't reattach an ear. Well, at the Teddy Bears' picnic, there were all kinds of very nice big people who were doctors and nurses, and they were there to make the teddy bears better. It was not only the teddy bears who needed help. I also saw several bunnies, dinosaurs, cats, dogs and even a stuffed pig who looked like he had eaten too much. The pig seemed to be very much loved by the little girl who had brought him to the picnic, and the doctors were able to repair his detaching tail.

We took my teddy bear to the ear doctor, and the doctor joked with him to calm him. My teddy bear was reassured and gave his consent to the treatment. At first I thought I wouldn't look because of the needles and scissors, but the doctor helped me calm down by asking me if I thought my teddy bear had a bunny in his ear. It's funny how sometimes a crazy idea can help you through a difficult moment. My teddy bear was fine once his detaching ear was back in its original place, and to reward him for not having bitten the nice doctor, I had a cast put on his leg.

After his operation, my teddy bear needed some food, so Mommy and Daddy bought me an ice cream cone. I offered a bite to my teddy bear, but he doesn't like chocolate ice cream, so he just drank some water instead. Afterwards, we played games with the other children and their animals and listened to some musicians who were making lovely music. Then we went home because all picnics must end with a good nap.

A few days later, my mommy explained to me that I would need to go to see an ear doctor. One of my ears was blocked with water, and the doctor would unblock it. I asked her if I would see the ear doctor who had treated my teddy bear. Mommy said probably not, because the teddy bear doctor specialized in reattaching detaching ears, and my ear was in absolutely no danger of becoming detached. She assured me that I could discuss things with the doctor and that I would know when to give my consent to treatment. My ear doctor works in a hospital, so that's where we went to meet him. You probably know what hospitals are and what they do, as they are all over the city so I don't have to explain all that to you. Let me just say that hospitals are strange places in the sense that you want them to be there, but you don't want to have to go in them. That's how I feel about my bed sometimes. I wouldn't want anyone to take it away, but I don't necessarily want to go in it, especially in the afternoon.

So we went to the hospital. Mommy recommended that I bring my crocodile, as going to the hospital can be quite an adventure. And so can getting water pumped out of your ear. I must admit I wasn't crazy about the water-pumping thing. Grandma once gave me a book where you can see inside people's bodies. It shows that people are full of all kinds of water. I wondered just how much of the water would be pumped out through my ear. But that didn't worry me for long because the doctor explained that it would be a very tiny, tiny drop, and he made a little dot on a paper with a pencil to show me. I won't bore you with details of the pumping session. Let's just say that I didn't appreciate it at all and that my crocodile and I made sure the doctor understood this.

When I felt better, Mommy, who is good at recognizing that I have been put through a lot – even though she is sometimes precisely the one who puts me through a lot – took me for a snack at the hospital cafeteria. I had oatmeal cookies with some chocolate in them. (I don't think you can get a full chocolate cookie in a hospital.) Then Mommy said we would go and visit her friend Tracey, who works with the children who have a bed in that hospital, and that Tracey would show us around. We took a very big elevator and I got to drive it. Tracey and Mommy hugged each other and said it had been too long, and Tracey walked with us so we could meet other nurses and some of the children. I rather liked the way the hospital is decorated. The colours are very bright, and there are many drawings made by the children who have a bed in the hospital.

We got to see many children, but we talked to only a couple of them. The others were in their beds having some water pumped backed into them, as I could see by the tubes going into their bodies. Other children had invited their parents to visit them and were playing games with them. Some children were in a big room and a nice lady was having them build things with playdough. I don't know exactly why, but I had a bit of a trembly tummy when I saw the children. One girl who was bigger than me said I was cute and would I like to build playdough cookies with her. I accepted, but at first I was a bit afraid of her because she had no hair at all and big cheeks. The only way I could tell she was a girl was that she was wearing a frilly pink T-shirt and also her name is Lucy. Lucy and I talked while making the cookies, and I discovered she knows all there is to know about trembly tummies. She has them quite often herself, she says, but she has several friends in the hospital who also understand about trembly tummies and they help her. Friends who understand about trembly tummies are like good crocodiles. I told Lucy all about my visit to the ear doctor, and she understood what it means when you have to do things that you don't want to do or are afraid of. She showed me her bed, which is in a room with other beds full of children, but they are not allowed to have pillow fights. And then because she had really enjoyed my visit, she gave me a card that she had received which has clowns and balloons on it. Lucy said a used card is even better than a new card because a card picks up love and good wishes each time it goes to a new person.

We said goodbye to Lucy and Tracey. I drove the elevator once again, and while I was busy doing that, I realized that my tummy was not trembly anymore. My crocodile was sleeping peacefully in my pocket and I let him, as he was not needed immediately. My mommy just transferred both of us from the car to my bed for our naps.

Grandma was glad when I told her this story. Any story that involves teddy bears, children and me is of great interest to her. She says she learns a lot from me and I am proud to help her in that way. She wasn't surprised at all that Lucy and I had enjoyed the time we spent together. She couldn't say exactly who started the enjoyment. Perhaps it was me, because I was quickly able to see Lucy as a fun person to play with rather than a sick child who has no hair and big cheeks. Maybe it was Lucy, because she found me cute and felt she could give me something by doing playdough with me. Sometimes sick children forget how much they can and do give to all around them. The big people may forget it, too. Maybe it was both of us at the same time who started the enjoyment; it doesn't matter at all. What Grandma understood is that I was able to see Lucy as she *is*, as opposed to what she *has*. Lucy was able to see me as a cute little boy who was having an adventure and not as a little child who had cried at the doctor's office and didn't know how lucky he was that his only problem was water in his ear. According to Grandma, real joy between persons comes when the persons look at each other to try to figure out who the other person is. Of course, they will never really know who the other person is because the heart of another person is always a mystery. It is the trying to know that is important, not the actual knowing.

Maybe what Grandma was saying is not completely clear to you. If that is so, one of two things can be done about this. The first one is that I could arrange for you to meet my grandma, and you could ask her directly what she means about this. The other one is that you keep on looking at what Grandma says till you understand in your very own way. I am quite certain that Grandma would say that the second method is by far the most interesting. Grandma also had an idea about what happens to children who have a bed in the hospital. She says that they are observed, very often, by many people, who try to figure out what's happening to them. All those people talk about the children, hoping to find a way to help them get better, and very often the children do get better. The people who help the children know how important observing a child is. But, Grandma says, all the big people in the world should learn to observe all children carefully to understand what's happening to them. In other words, children don't have to be sick to be placed under close observation. It has been proven that closely observed children get better even if they are not even sick.

This certainly gave me the opportunity to remind Grandma that we hadn't closely observed Prince Igor in quite a while. So Grandma had me close my eyes to find where Prince Igor was at this time. I discovered that he is now travelling by the seashore and collecting seashells so his camel can listen to the sounds of the ocean. I noticed that the camel's ear is detaching a little bit, and I asked Grandma if there was such a thing as a Camels' Picnic. Grandma said she would find out, and if there isn't such a thing, we could organize one.

"Today is a good day"

Today is a good day.

No tests, no new procedures

No needles, no drug-induced sleeps.

So you've requested that I bring

what used to be your favourite movie

A long time ago –

The one with that fish with the defective fin

And his overanxious daddy.

I look at you, totally absorbed in the story
And I feel the terrible split in me.
Your illness has cut me in half,
Right down the middle of my mind and my heart.
On one side, the terror, the pain, the rage,
      the hopelessness;
On the other, the hope, the discovery, the courage,
      your smile.
My two sides are not touching each other.
They are not even on speaking terms
And I never know which will be the one
That will answer the dreaded question
"And how is your little guy doing?"

"Skip that part, Daddy. Go to my favourite part,"
you command.
"The part where the strange animals dance."
Your face lights up and you start making
that funny sound
That used to make you laugh and dance
through the room.
"Hey, hey, hey, hey! Hey, hey, hey, hey!"
You move your skinny arms and head in rhythm
And the dance makes you tumble into peals of laughter.
"Isn't dancing fun, Daddy?"
I grab you into a big hug
My hands and arms join behind your back
And I feel whole once more.

21

Joining a church:

A baptism

Recently I had the honour of being invited to go into a church. Some of you may already know about churches, but some of you may not, so I'll explain briefly how you can recognize a church and even go into one in cities that are full of buildings. Let me make it easy for you to spot a church. In a city, buildings that are not houses, stores, hospitals or train stations are churches. It's that simple.

As for going into a church, it's a little more complicated, but it can be done with a bit of luck or a bit of daring. If you are lucky, someone will invite you into their church, and then you can get to see all the candles and listen to some nice singing. If you are not lucky, you have to invite yourself to go into your chosen church, and that requires some daring because once you are inside, there are no friends to help you find your way around and explain things. Among other things, churches can have some very dark corners. They are built this way to make sure that people can rest in peace when they need to.

I got lucky. Friends of my mommy and daddy invited us to go to church with them to see their new babies and welcome them into the community. Teresa and Robert are the names of the parents of the new babies. Instead of having one baby, they had two at the same time – that is what we call twins. The two babies are built exactly alike and Daddy said it was very difficult to tell them apart. I can't see why: one is dressed in blue, the other one in yellow. It's easy to tell which is which. Twins are very practical to have around the house. If one of them is crying, you can play with the other one. On the day I went into the church, the twins were not crying – at least not until the man and the woman poured water all over their heads, but I'll come to that later. The babies had been invited to come into the church to meet their community. A community is a bunch of people who get together to help each other and then have a party. It's very important for people to belong to a community, as belonging to a community can help you grow strong and healthy. It's even better when people belong to several communities, according to Grandma.

The twins' community was already gathered in the church when we arrived, and the people had started to have some kind of a party, even though they had not yet helped each other. I guess they are allowed to have a party before the help part if they promise to really help afterwards. The people were laughing and saying "hello" to each other and "isn't this a lovely occasion." After a while we all sat down on the benches, which are a bit like park benches but all lined up one behind the other. My parents and I sat right in front so we could see the action. The action started with some music and singing, and then Teresa talked to the community. By that time, I had understood that I was part of the community, having been invited into the church. I was happy about that because I like listening to music and singing. I was also hoping, though, that this community included food in its parties. So Teresa thanked us for being there with the twins, and she thanked us for the gifts the community had brought. I looked around to see the gifts, but I couldn't see them. I like gifts even if they are not for me, though of course I prefer it when they are. I always offer to help with the unwrapping. I'm very good at it. So I discreetly asked my Daddy where the gifts were, and Daddy said he would explain later. I thought maybe they had been put in one of the dark corners – not the best choice for gifts, if you ask me. Everybody looked happy about the gifts, and they even applauded each other. I joined in because I like applauding. It makes me look as if I understand what is going on.

Meanwhile, the babies were sleeping in their car seats and not meeting the community, so Teresa and Robert picked them up and showed them to everyone. Everybody applauded. Applauding is something people in a church like to do, apparently. Then everybody left his or her seat and we gathered around a wishing well. I know all about wishing wells, as they are in many storybooks. This wishing well was like a really big bowl made of stone, and there was some water in it. Teresa and Robert invited the people to make good wishes for the babies, so many people spoke to say they hoped the babies would grow well and have a nice life. The twins were put back into their car seats because that part was quite long. After a while, I became a bit bored with all the good wishes, and I started feeling a bit sleepy.

Then a man and a woman, dressed in long white dresses that went right down to their shoes, invited Teresa and Robert to pick up their babies again and hold on tight to them. Well, holding on tight to the babies was good advice because the man and the woman dressed in white took water from the well and poured it right over the babies' heads. The yellow twin almost jumped out of his skin, he was so shocked. Jumping out of your skin means that you are so surprised about something that you feel that your skin has stopped holding you together. He completely woke up and started crying. The blue twin also understood that something really strange was going on, and he started crying, too. I would even say that he started shrieking. Teresa and Robert dried the babies' heads with a towel, rubbed their backs and made soothing sounds to them, as if they weren't the ones who had let the babies get their heads wet in the first place. The twins are Teresa and Robert's first children, so they have no idea what babies like or hate.

After the twins were dried and calmed down, the man and the woman in the white dresses announced to the community that they would now tell us the names of the twins. But before that, they suggested that we all take a moment or two to think of our own name and be grateful to the people who had gone to the trouble of giving us a nice name. Then they said that every time a person says our name, he or she touches us. Because of that, we should all be careful of how we say other people's names. The way we say their name can feel very nice to them, like a tickle with a feather or not so nice, like a pinch on the heart. Then they told us the names of the twins. I think the yellow twin got the best name, but both names are very fine names, so if the twins ever get mixed up and nobody knows which is which, it won't really matter.

Then there was some more singing and praying. When people all talk together and say exactly the same words, it's called praying. If all the people were saying the words one after the other, it would take far too long and the Listener would lose interest. Praying is a really great idea. It saves time. Then we were invited to the basement of the church for some sandwiches and cake. I thought I might find the gifts down there, but they weren't there. So while Daddy and I were having some cake, I asked him once again about the gifts. He explained that the gifts had already been given; that's why I could not see them here. The other reason I couldn't see them is that they were sort of invisible. What happened is this: Teresa and Robert saw that they had all the clothes and furniture they needed for the twins, so they asked the community for a special gift. They asked the people to give a little bit of time and a little bit of love to other communities. Communities must welcome babies, and that's what we were doing with the twins today. But communities themselves need help to be able to continue to do their work of helping others. So Teresa and Robert asked all the people to think of what the twins and all other babies in the world would need as they grow up, and to give a little bit of time and love to the communities that help babies, young children and big children. That would be our gift to the twins.

Daddy knew one woman who thought that winters in our country are very cold, so she decided to help with the snowsuit fund, which tries to make sure every young child has a snowsuit of a good colour. A couple of people thought that the twins or other children might have bad luck and have problems finding a place to live when they grow up, so they gave some time to the shelter for people with a house problem. A woman thought that the twins or other children might have problems with their hearing, so she signed up to learn how to speak with her fingers to be able to help deaf people. A man thought that children and adults need to read to learn things about the world and themselves, so he decided to help make sure books get read many times by different people. A woman and her husband thought the twins or other children might be sick one day, so they decided to help decorate the children's hospital with really nice pictures to cheer up the children who have a bed in the hospital. All kinds of things like that.

I asked my daddy what gift he had given. He answered that Mommy and he thought that the twins or other children might one day have the bad luck to be hungry and not have food, so they had been volunteering at the food bank for the past few weeks. He said it was their way of saying thank you for the fact that they had enough food for me. So that is what the gifts were. It was the strangest kind of gifts I had ever heard of, but my tummy felt quite happy for the twins and Teresa and Robert.

I couldn't wait to tell Grandma all about my adventure at the church. She especially liked this one because she likes stories about communities where people help each other. She thought Teresa and Robert were very generous and creative people. She also said that the twins, though they didn't know it, had given many people the opportunity to learn new things and spread love in the world. She added that little children do that all the time by the fact that they really need big people to love them and care for them. That is why babies keep coming into the world. The human race needs them to continue to learn and grow.

Grandma was glad that I had enjoyed the experience of going into a church. She believes that churches are very special places because people go to a church when they want to think about Life and God, which are pretty much the same thing as far as she is concerned. Going into a church can provide quiet time to be grateful to Life and God and think about how you can help Life and God be even more abundant. Sometimes a church does not provide quiet time because it is full of people celebrating something special, like the twins' birth, but this is good noise. It is the noise of people coming together to help each other and say that they care for each other. Both quietness and noise are good in a church.

Grandma said that there are many different kinds of churches and she hopes that as I grow older I will get to know at least a few of them. I will then be able to decide which one will help me grow best. According to Grandma, I will grow all my life, even when my bones have stopped growing and I am officially a big person. Grandma added that after a while I can even decide to change churches if I discover that another one would be best for me. She recommended, however, that I steer clear of people who insist that their church is the only good one for all humankind. That kind of thinking can create war instead of peace, understanding and Life.

Grandma also told me that when I am older and don't need to nap so often, I can go back into a church as often as I want. But in the meantime I can invite a church to go into me. That seemed a bit weird to me at first, but as Grandma has explained, a church is supposed to be a quiet place so people can find answers to their questions and learn to embrace the great mysteries of Life. So when I need to find a quiet place during my life, I may invite a church to come into me.

Grandma and I decided to see what Prince Igor had been doing since we last caught sight of him. It turned out he was quietly sitting by a campfire that he had built to keep himself and his camel warm. You might not know this, but the desert can be a very cold place during the night, even though the sun can burn you during the day. Prince Igor was sitting very still because he was finding some warmth inside of him also. Prince Igor has been travelling for a very long time now, and sometimes when you travel alone your heart gets cold. The fire helped him remember that he would one day find his teddy bear.

"Let us pray to God, said the priest"

Let us pray to God, said the priest,

For all those parents

And all those children

Who do not take the time to pray.

The parents find the time

To wash, clean and scrub

To cook, bake and serve

To console, soothe and dry tears

To nurse, support and listen.

They take the time to give love all day long.

Why is it that they do not take the time to pray?

The children find the time

To run, jump and climb

To pretend, imagine and invent

To dance, laugh and sing

To walk, learn and grow.

They take the time to receive love all day long.

Why is it that they do not take the time to pray?

Let us pray to me, said God

For the hard-working and hard-praying priest

Who has not yet understood

That the parents who give love

And the children who receive love

Are softly praying all day long.

Over the centuries, said God,

I have had the time to listen

To countless hard prayers

Sent to me by humankind –

Yes, the very same humankind

That can behave in the worst possible way.

And though only those closest to me might suspect it,

I am quite tired and fed-up at times.

I have become a thin-skinned God,

And hard prayers irritate me no end.

So please, somebody out there,

Spread the word to all humankind

That the only prayers I truly enjoy

Are the soft ones.

May I kindly request that you send no other kind?

22

Discovering the richness of life:

Food

I may have mentioned before that I really enjoy chocolate cake. Grandma says that chocolate cake brings out the best in me. She notices that I behave quite well in the presence of chocolate cake. I have to agree with her. Chocolate cake is something that comes and goes in my life. If I want to help it come to me and go into my tummy, I find it useful to be very polite and resist all temptations related to throwing. Chocolate cake is well worth that effort. As a matter of fact, chocolate cake is so nice that you barely notice that it is food.

It gives me great joy to talk about chocolate cake, but food in general is not something I would care to talk about. Food does not always contain great joy, and food in general does not always bring out the best in me. But Grandma has invited me to discuss food because it is such an important subject for the whole of humankind. So I've decided to share some of my thoughts with you. Grandma will like this because she has these dreams of the earth being a great big garden where everybody would grow good vegetables that even children could appreciate and everybody could share. I like doing things to please Grandma, even if she has never provided me with chocolate cake. She does, however, have Prince Igor eat some when he travels for a long while. It brings out the best in him. I figure that it is a small jump from Prince Igor to me. Perhaps Grandma will surprise me one day.

My friends and I discuss food occasionally because when food is served in a group, you can either discuss food or have some kind of fight over it. All the adults I know, and I know about eleventeen hundred, strongly prefer food discussions to food fights, and all the adults encourage children to deal with food in a civilized manner. A civilized manner means you must say thanks for the food you are being fed, even if you have no idea if it is food that you actually would be thankful for. It means you must keep your fork on your plate when it is not in your mouth. It means you must taste everything that is presented to you, though there is no guarantee that this particular food is fit for consumption by a child. It also means you are not allowed to put your feet on the table. These are the basic rules, the ones that are taught to children all over the world. A basic rule is a rule that if you don't obey it, you might get hurt. If you run into the street, you might get hurt. If you refuse to taste your food, you might get hurt, because not having dessert can hurt quite a bit. There are many other rules around food, and it seems that all families have their own set of rules. Martin, my friend who has two daddies, two brothers, two houses, but only one dog, gets to have to obey two sets of rules because every week, he moves from one house to the other. Sometimes he forgets which house he is in exactly, and the rules get mixed up. In one house, he's allowed to eat while watching TV. In the other house, this is considered very bad manners. Poor Martin keeps forgetting which is which. But that doesn't really matter, as Martin is good at dealing with rules. He once taught me a good rule trick: if you don't like a new rule, just pretend you haven't heard it. This way, you can't get a time out because one of the rules of time outs is that the child has to understand why he is being given a time out. That is an excellent trick, and it worked for a whole day at my house.

Food can create the occasion to get quite a few fights going. Some fights happen at daycare because, as Denise likes to say, this is not a restaurant, and you can't all have different menus. It happened once that I sort of started a food fight there. When Connor wasn't looking, I put a piece of my broccoli in his plate to help him grow strong bones. It seems that Connor doesn't want strong bones because he threw the broccoli right across the kitchen and it landed on Denise's magazine. To make matters worse, Connor also started shrieking. Why he started shrieking, I have no idea. The broccoli had never even touched his mouth. Denise didn't appreciate Connor's behaviour at all, but for some reason that I don't quite understand, I was the one who was made to take a moment of reflection. This is another expression for a time out.

My friends and I agree that food can be quite a hassle, and we have occasionally discussed how to handle parents who have food problems. Most of our parents do have food problems. They work hard to make us healthy food, and they worry when we don't eat all our vegetables. They can get really upset when we don't get excited about things like tofu and whole-grain bread without additives. I'll have you notice that most people don't even know what tofu is made of, yet they seem happy enough. Children don't like it when their parents are upset because the parents' upsetness can spill over and fall on the children, and then everybody is sort of upside down, especially their tummies. So children must try to make their parents relax about food. It's not easy because feeding their children is the most important thing parents must do, and I am beginning to understand that it's very hard and complex work. I must ask Grandma why this is. I'm not certain she has any kind of experience with feeding young children, but that won't stop her from inventing a good answer.

At this point, I will share a trick to help with food issues. If you are worried about what's going into your food, a good way to get some control over the situation is to offer to help prepare the food. Food that you have prepared yourself always tastes good, except for the few times it doesn't. I like it when my mommy asks me to do some of the cooking. It gives her a break, and she can concentrate on the cleaning up without worrying about the actual food. I am a good cook, if I may say so myself. I can give you my recipe for eggs "Ariane," if you wish. Ariane is my cousin, and she is really inventive with eggs. Just make sure you have at least one egg more than is required for the recipe.

I knew Grandma would be very interested in explaining why food can become such a complicated issue in families. She likes food and she likes families, so of course she has thought a lot about the subject. She thinks that all the people in the world, even those we have never met, all belong to the same family, and therefore must grow their food together and share it so everybody gets to be well fed. The larger a family is, of course, the more difficult it is to agree on things, and Grandma admits that the large earth family has not yet worked out its food problems.

Grandma thinks that parents tend to worry about food because they know on some level that they are doing much more than feeding children to help them grow healthy bones. They are teaching them about relationships as they are providing food, and relationships are often very complicated.

The first relationship is the one you have with your own being. In the case of food, your being is your tummy and your ideas. Parents sometimes forget that their children's tummies and ideas will tell them when they need food or have eaten enough food or when a certain food is not called for. When parents forget that, they feel they have to tell you to eat another piece of carrot, as if your tummy and your ideas weren't able to figure out when you have eaten enough. When your parents do your tummy's job, your tummy can become very lazy, and so can your ideas. After a while, your tummy and your ideas stop telling you things about food, and then you are stuck with listening to what everybody else says about food for the rest of your life. According to Grandma, parents tend to work too hard and forget that their children are good little animals. Sometimes they get carried away by their work and don't find time to relax a little. A good place to practise being relaxed about food is with broccoli.

The second relationship is the one you have with the whole earth. Grandma really likes to bring the whole earth into our discussions. I think that is why she makes Prince Igor travel to the faraway lands. According to Grandma, parents must make their children prepare for their relationship with the whole earth, so they make them practise at home. Food is apparently one of the best tools to practise all we have to know to make our way in the world. I was very surprised to learn about this, as I thought that food was only for eating. But Grandma knows her stuff, and even when she doesn't, you couldn't tell the difference, she's so good at it. So I'm telling it exactly like it is.

According to Grandma, food teaches us to *give*. That's what my parents do when they provide food for me.

Food teaches us to *receive and be grateful.* That is why I thank my mommy and daddy when they give me my plate.

Food teaches us to *share.* That's why my parents put some food in the food bank box at the grocery store.

Food teaches us to *enjoy simple pleasures.* That's why there is chocolate cake.

Food teaches us to *work.* That's why my parents let me help with the meal.

Food teaches us to *accept.* That's why I can't always have the food I want, all the time.

Food teaches us to *have respect.* I do that when I listen to what my tummy and ideas have to say about food. I do that also when I don't waste food.

Food teaches us to *be creative.* That's why my parents invent all kinds of recipes and tricks to help me enjoy my food and eat well.

Food teaches us to *ask.* I do that when I ask for seconds.

Food teaches us *to experiment and try new things and make mistakes.* That's why my parents occasionally throw away a recipe and vow never to serve that dish again.

Food teaches us to *express our ideas and feelings.* That's why I say that food is sometimes "yummy" and sometimes "yucky." It's all right to say these things, but not all right to throw my food on the floor to show that I don't like it.

Food teaches us to *make choices.* That's why my mommy asks me what kind of cereal I would like this morning.

Food teaches us to *refuse.* I do that when I say, "No, thank you."

And when I have learned all these things, even very imperfectly, I will be ready to venture out into the world and travel the earth to give and receive Love. And that is when Prince Igor will finally find his teddy bear.

All of this according to Grandma.

"We sit facing
each other"

We sit facing each other.

I am trying to be patient with you.

You are trying to be patient with me.

I want you to understand that these vegetables,

Prepared with love and knowledge of nutrition,

Will help you grow strong bones

And therefore are good for you.

You want me to understand that this gooey stuff

Will turn you into a green-skinned monster

And therefore is bad for you.

Your eyes unlock from mine and take on
        this unfocused look,
which indicates that you are not listening to me.
Perhaps you are gazing into a future where you
        will get to choose
what you want to eat and when and how and where
        and why.
Meanwhile, I gaze into a hopefully very distant future
where I am old and frail and about to embark
        on a new Life adventure.
My grandchildren have gathered to hear my last words
        of wisdom,
which I must keep very short, as I am running out
        of breath.

I would like to tell my grandchildren to make
        good food choices:
To choose what feeds them well, physically
        and spiritually.
To choose what makes them grow tall and strong
        and loving.
To choose to make choices and dare change them.

I would like to tell my grandchildren to take very good
        care of their choices:
To support them, embrace them and cherish them.
I would like to tell them always to honour their choices
And do them well.

But to say all this would be too long for
       my feeble breathing,
So I just look lovingly at my dear grandchildren
       and whisper,
"choose your food and feed your choices."